孫子兵法

To the late Keith Westphal (1950–2003),
my best man, good friend, and fellow salesman

孫子兵法

孫子兵法

Sun Tzu's
THE
ART
OF
WAR

Plus
Book Series

The Art of Sales
Strategy for Salespeople

孫 子 兵 法

Sun Tzu's
THE
ART
OF
WAR

Plus
Book Series

The Art of Sales
Strategy for Salespeople

by Gary Gagliardi

Clearbridge Publishing

Published by
Clearbridge Publishing

SECOND HARDCOVER EDITION, second printing
Copyright 1999, 2001, 2003, 2004 Gary Gagliardi

Manufactured in the United States of America.
Interior and cover graphic design by Dana and Jeff Wincapaw.
Original Chinese calligraphy by Tsai Yung, Green Dragon Arts, www.greendragonarts.com.

Publisher's Cataloging-in-Publication Data
Sun-tzu, 6th cent. B.C.
    [Sun-tzu ping fa, English]
    The art of war plus the art of sales / Sun Tzu and Gary Gagliardi.
    p. 192 cm. 23
    Includes introduction to basic competitive philosophy of Sun Tzu
    ISBN 1-929194-35-8 (hbk.) ISBN 1-929194-01-3 (pbk.)
    1. Selling. 2. Sales management. 3. Sales promotion. 4. Military art and science - Early works
to 1800. I. Gagliardi, Gary 1951— . II. The Art of Sales
HF5438.5.S86 1999
658.8 /1 21 —dc21

                        Library of Congress Catalog Card Number: 99-64138

Clearbridge Publishing's books may be purchased for business, for any promotional use,
or for special sales. Please contact:

Clearbridge
Clearbridge Publishing
PO Box 33772, Seattle, WA 98133
Phone: (206)533-9357 Fax: (206)546-9756
www.clearbridge.com

Contents

The Art of War Plus
The Art of Sales

Foreword

Using Strategy in Sales

The purpose of this book is to make it easy to apply the ancient strategic principles of Sun Tzu's *The Art of War* to selling. How does *The Art of War* apply to making sales? To borrow from the German general Karl von Clausewitz, selling is war by other means. In writing his book, Sun Tzu foresaw that the competition would move into other arenas. He described the grounds on which war can be fought as "infinite." In his work, he never mentions the types of weapons or forces used in war because he saw that strategy can be used in many different areas and that, at its heart, all competition is economic. In many ways, today's competing businesses resemble the contesting city-states of Sun Tzu's era—in scale and psychology—much more than our nation-states do.

The Art of War offers a strategy that will win you more and larger sales more quickly. Sun Tzu's strategic principles teach that only a few key factors influence the outcome of your efforts. These factors are easily adapted to selling. In sales and Sun Tzu's strategy, success goes not to the most aggressive but to those who best understand their situation and what their alternatives really are. When you have mastered Sun Tzu's system of strategy, you will be able to almost instantly analyze sales situations, spot sales opportunities, and make the appropriate decisions.

In our adaptation for salespeople, the rules of strategy are tailored to help you in your role as a communicator and persuader.

孫
子
兵
法

You will find that Sun Tzu's lessons work especially well in strategic sales to organizations. They work when selling to middle managers and top decision-makers. Since we have other specific adaptations for managing, marketing, career building, and small business, this work concentrates on working with buyers and decision-makers. The challenges include analyzing your sales situation, planning a proposal, adjusting to a customer's specific needs, diagnosing a prospect's behavior, and so on. As a salesperson, you have to face a wide variety of issues, and we try to address a broad spectrum of them in this work.

As in all our *Art of War Plus* books, we present our sales version side by side with our complete translation of the original text of *The Art of War*. We suggest that in reading this work, you read both texts and not just our sales adaptation. Our English translation of the original Chinese uses military terminology to capture Sun Tzu's ideas. However, the original Chinese concepts are not limited to military applications. The sales text is not based on our English translation but on the original Chinese, and it demonstrates the different ways rules of strategy can be applied. Sun Tzu's underlying concepts are rich and complex. The relationships among these basic principles are explained in the INTRODUCTION, which follows.

The Art of Sales is a different type of book on selling. It addresses sales strategy in its most critical form. It won't give you any tricks for overcoming objections or clever phrases for closing a sale. There are plenty of books that address those techniques. Instead, this book focuses on the long-term issues. It teaches the kind of thinking, planning, and decision-making that it takes to have a successful career in selling.

The book first addresses large-scale issues in selling that other books usually overlook. Do you understand the importance and challenges of a career in sales? Are you committed to it? Are you working for the right company and selling the right products?

These topics are addressed in the beginning chapters of the text. You cannot be successful in sales unless you are the right person selling the right products for the right reason. As you read deeper into the book, the text delves into a variety of more specific situations and special conditions that help you with the specific sales process that you might be engaged in.

The Art of Sales converts Sun Tzu's ideas from the military arena to the world of the salesperson as consistently as possible. We start by defining selling as a battle for the customer's mind. The nation for whom the army fights becomes the company for whom the salesperson sells. Winning the battle means getting the order.

In Sun Tzu's view, the secret to warfare is not just winning battles. It is winning quickly and economically. You must keep what you have won. Victory alone is not enough. Sun Tzu teaches that true success is "making victory pay," that is, making victory profitable and rewarding. You must be wary of costly "victories" that consume your time and energy but fail to bring you long-term success in building a territory.

This concept of victory maps extremely well onto any intelligent view of sales. Your purpose isn't just to get orders; it is to win and keep customers. It is to win sales quickly and effortlessly. You want to win in a way that leaves you ready for the next sale, not so burnt out that you need a vacation.

In creating a sales adaptation of Sun Tzu's work, the biggest challenge is in defining who "the enemy" is. Sometimes the enemy is a competitor who is trying to win away your customers. More often, however, you are engaged in a contest of wills with your prospects, the people to whom you are trying to sell. This raises the question: Is the customer really "the enemy"?

Strangely enough, Sun Tzu's unique view of warfare makes this problem less difficult to resolve than it might seem at first. Sun Tzu sees the enemy as a partner in warfare. All competitors work with their enemies to make victory possible. In the original Chinese, the character translated into English as "enemy" is often the character for "nobleman," that is, a decision-maker. *The Art of War* does not teach an aggressive or antagonistic view of competition, but rather a cooperative one. Sun Tzu's methods teach you to set up situations in which conflict is unnecessary and the enemy—that is, your customer—very naturally surrenders.

This interpretation reflects any salesperson's natural preoccupation with the customer and the customer's thinking. Only occasionally do Sun Tzu's ideas about the enemy apply to your direct competitors. As a salesperson, you must know what your competitors are doing, but only occasionally should you take action directed at your competitors. Customers, not competitors, determine your fate. To use this book successfully, you have to appreciate customers and competitors and the roles that they play in your success.

You will be intrigued by the lessons that emerge when *bing-fa* is applied to make sales.

First, Sun Tzu teaches that having a solid sales process is not good enough. You must learn to think competitively. Your prospects have many other ways to spend their money. You win sales for one reason: you present decision-makers with the best possible alternative for investing their money.

Second, an essential ingredient of success is picking the right battleground, or, in our sales adaptation, highlighting the right issues in the buying decision. As a salesperson, you must focus the sales process on the customer problems that your product or service, and only *your* product or service, can properly address.

Third, you must also continually innovate. In Sun Tzu's terms, you must always adapt to the changes that take place on the field of battle, but this does not mean that you can abandon proven sales processes and techniques. According to the principles of *bing-fa*, standards (or the existing sales process) lead to innovation and innovation leads to new standards. You must broaden your standard sales process so that it better fits a wider variety of specific customer problems.

Next, you must be opportunistic. According to Sun Tzu's teaching, you cannot succeed through your own actions alone. You don't create opportunities. You can defend your existing position from attack, but the competitive environment itself must provide the opportunities for organizational success. The secret is recognizing these opportunities when they present themselves, and, once you recognize them, you must have the confidence to act. Selling often requires watchful patience. At other times, selling requires instant action. Sun Tzu argues that opportunities are always abundant, since every problem creates an opportunity, but that they can be difficult to recognize and act upon.

Finally, Sun Tzu's view of competition is knowledge-intensive. He sees victory going to the person who is the most knowledgeable. Sun Tzu's focus on information is so clear that he devotes his final chapter, USING SPIES, to it. In the sales version, this chapter is adapted as USING QUESTIONS. In Sun Tzu's system, there is no substitute for good information. Knowledge means having better information than anyone else. For a salesperson, it means knowing more about your area of business than any of your competitors know.

The universal utility of strategy means that you can apply its rules in different ways in different situations. For this reason, you should read and reread Sun Tzu's work at least once a year. With every reading, you will develop more insight into Sun Tzu's methods and your own situation. As your situation changes, different parts of the book will become more important. In general, the book is organized so that the broadest and longest-term issues, such as strategic planning, are addressed in the initial chapters. Later chapters tend to focus on the special challenges encountered under specific conditions. Despite its relatively short length, this book contains more valuable information about good sales practices than other books two or three times its size. Do not expect to appreciate all of its principles in one reading. Time spent studying Sun Tzu's system is always time well invested.

Reading and rereading this book is simply the first step in mastering the warrior's world of competitive philosophy. This book is a simplification of Sun Tzu's strategic system. His complete system is sophisticated and deep. Much of its sophistication is not readily apparent simply from reading the text. This sales adaptation helps you use Sun Tzu's ideas easily, but if you are interested in mastering the art of strategy, we offer a host of material to make it easy.

Our Mastering Strategy series starts with *Sun Tzu's The Art of War Plus The Ancient Chinese Revealed*, which shows the Chinese formulas of the original text and allows you to see the limitations of any English translation. The next book in the series, *Sun Tzu's The Art of War Plus Its Amazing Secrets,* explains the strategic concepts in detail. It reveals the hidden aspects of the text and diagrams out Sun Tzu's system. The final book in the series is *The Art of War Plus The Warrior Class: 306 Lessons in Strategy*. This book transforms Sun Tzu's work into a series of lessons on strategy.

We also offer a number of audio, video, in-person, and on-line training tools. We suggest you visit www.BooksOnStrategy.com for a complete overview of the training in strategy that we offer.

孫子兵法

Heaven

Battle

Moving

Deception

Foreseeing

Uniting

Methods

Philosophy

Leader

Division

Positioning

Focusing

Knowing

Siege

Surprise

Ground

Introduction

The Sales Strategist

This book teaches using classical strategy to achieve success in selling. To put you on the path of the sales strategist, let us clarify the use of Sun Tzu's strategic system. Sun Tzu did not write his book to train the uninitiated. In his era, people learned directly from a living master. Books were supplements. They were designed for study after the basic concepts, metaphors, and analogies were well understood. Because of this, the text of *The Art of War* is difficult for the new readers to grasp easily. The purpose of this introduction is explain its basic principles.

The difference between sales strategists and regular salespeople is their reactions to challenges. Our instinctual reaction to a challenge is either "flight" or "fight," running away or getting into conflict. This is how most salespeople react to the inevitable obstacles put in their way by customers and competitors. Salespeople close their eyes to these obstacles or argue against them. Sales strategists react differently because they are given a set of tools to analyze their situation and a larger set of responses from which to choose. Sales strategists are much more likely to go around obstacles, ignore them, or use them than to argue against them.

Sun Tzu's strategic tool kit for analysis is based on the *five element system* introduced in the first section of his first chapter. These five elements—philosophy, heaven, earth, the leader, and methods—define a strategic position and provide the backbone of strategic analysis. All the other components of his system—deception, unity, knowledge, and so on—have very specific and logical relationships to these five elements. The depth and sophistication of the system require some explanation.

Sun Tzu taught that every competitive situation depends upon the unique position of a given competitor within the larger competitive environment. Strategy is focused on building up or advancing your position in such a way that opponents cannot attack you and ideally others want to join you. In choosing between your product and a competitor's, the customer decides based upon your relative positions within this larger competitive environment.

The focus on the competitive environment was a unique feature of Sun Tzu's work, at least until Darwin. As with so many of Sun Tzu's basic concepts, he describes the environment as two opposite and yet complementary halves, *heaven (sky)* and *earth (ground)*. Heaven and earth are the arenas of time and place within which you compete vying for your customers' dollars.

Heaven represents the uncontrollable passage of time, but more accurately it describes change. It is often translated as the "climate" or "weather" in the text. It is best to think of heaven as trends that change over time. As the realm of the gods, heaven is beyond our control. Weather and the cycle of the seasons are the most obvious aspects of changing heaven. People's attitudes and emotions are also an important part of Sun Tzu's concept of heaven. In the salesperson's environment, economic trends, product fashions, and business cycles cannot be controlled. The fact that these aspects of your situation change naturally is critically important.

Earth or ground is both where we fight and what we fight over. It is the territory in which the sales battle takes place. It is also the economic foundation that provides our financial support. As a salesperson, you can think of the earth or ground as your customer base. Unlike heaven, which is largely beyond our control, the most important aspect of the earth is that changes in ground result only from our choices and actions. You choose your customers. You choose what to say about your products and company. Choosing positions, moving to them, and utilizing them are the basis of Sun Tzu's strategic methods.

The first two components of your strategic position are your focus on a certain time and place, on heaven and earth.

Your company and its products are positioned within a *heaven* of changing market trends. Your product can be ahead of these trends or behind them. All products represent a prediction about what is important for the future. Your customers are making decisions today about what will be important in the future. All the emotions involved in the sales cycle are based upon the fears and uncertainties about what the future will bring.

Your strategic position is grounded on an *earth* of real customers. These customers are your base of financial support. You battle with competitors for the limited amount of money these customers are willing to spend. Correctly analyzing this ground and picking the right customers is the basis of your success.

Within the larger competitive environment, you and your company have certain unique characteristics. As he does with the environment, Sun Tzu breaks the important characteristics of a competitor into two opposite and competitive halves: the *leader* and *methods*.

As defined by Sun Tzu, all salespeople are leaders. The *leader* is a person who makes the decisions at the point of battle. Leadership is the realm of individual character. A leader masters the strategy so that he or she can make the right decisions quickly. By this definition, all customers are also leaders, that is, decision-makers.

Methods are the techniques of organization. Success depends upon working with other people. Methods are, by definition, the realm where we interact with other people. Salespeople make decisions as individuals, but it is the effect of those decisions upon other people, especially customers, that matters.

Binding and underlying your strategic position is its *philosophy*. *Philosophy* is the unique idea around which a specific strategic position is organized. In business, we call this a company mission or purpose. Philosophy is a shared goal. A core philosophy provides salespeople and their companies with unity and focus. Your philosophy also unites you with your customers. As a unifying force, philosophy is the beating heart of your strategic position.

The five elements defining your unique strategic position are the basis for understanding Sun Tzu's strategy.

You advance your strategic position using four external skills. These skills are *knowing, foreseeing, moving,* and *positioning.* A sales strategist's leadership depends on the skills of *knowing* and *foreseeing. Knowing* comes from understanding the competitive ground. Sales strategists must know their customers and potential customers. *Foreseeing* means recognizing the trends of heaven and that things are changing. A sales strategist must spot opportunities in change before others do. A sales strategist's methods depend on the skills of *moving* and *positioning* to work with others. *Moving* is changing positions to take advantage of opportunities. When you present your product or tackle an objection, you are moving the customer forward. *Positioning* is getting a reward for movement. All movement should generate benefits. One type of positioning is closing the sale.

These four external skills create an endless cycle of strategic positioning. Knowing leads to foreseeing. Our foresight dictates our moves. Moving gives us positioning. One of the rewards of positioning is more knowledge. For a sales strategist, keeping this cycle going, advancing his or her position, is the key to inevitable success. Unlike typical definitions of the sales cycle, this cycle has no endpoint. Even closing the sale is strategically a new beginning.

Sun Tzu also describes two internal skills: *uniting* and *focusing*. Though these concepts are separate in English, in Chinese they are the idea of "oneness." In Sun Tzu's system, both arise directly from the element of philosophy. Having the right philosophy unites sales strategists with their customers and focuses the sales cycle on both customer and company needs. Both determine your competitive *strength*. *Strength* is defined by the unity of a force, not its size.

Once you understand these internal and external skills, the many other aspects of strategy make more sense. There are five forms of attack, five weaknesses of leaders, six ways to evaluate strategic positions, six weaknesses of organizations, nine different strategic situations, and so on. All of these have specific relationships to the five elements that define a strategic position.

For example, Sun Tzu defines the five forms of attack. Strategically, an "attack" means advancing into an opponent's territory, not necessarily fighting. These five forms of attack—*surprise*, *deception*, *battle*, *siege*, and *division*—are aimed specifically at an opponent's skill. *Surprise* undermines knowledge. *Deception* spoils an opponent's foresight. *Battle* counters an opponent's motion. *Siege* tries to overturn a position. *Division* breaks up unity and focus. In many ways, these relationships define the nature of these attacks more precisely than the terms that we use.

For a picture of Sun Tzu's system of elements, skills, and attacks, you can refer to the diagram that precedes this introduction. This diagram summarizes Sun Tzu's methods in a traditional graphical map. Such maps were commonly used in all the sciences of ancient China. Sun Tzu's concepts are best understood within the context of these relationships in his complete system. A complete set of such diagrams for Sun Tzu's strategic concepts are provided in our book *Sun Tzu's The Art of War Plus Its Amazing Secrets*.

Heaven

Methods Philosophy Leader

Ground

Chapter 1

Analysis: Your Sales Position

Sales strategy begins with understanding your sales situation. Sun Tzu begins his book by giving instructions on how you evaluate your strategic position. For a salesperson, this form of strategic analysis is invaluable.

In the chapter's first part, Sun Tzu describes the five major components that define a competitive position—yours or your customers.

Then Sun Tzu describes how to directly compare your sales situation with that of your competitors'.

When you are in sales, it is hard to objectively look at your competitive position, so in the next section he stresses the importance of asking questions and getting outside viewpoints.

Sales is all about customer perceptions. The discussion in the following section moves to what Sun Tzu calls the use of deception. By "deception," Sun Tzu doesn't mean dishonesty—on the contrary, honesty is one of the necessary characteristics of a leader. His idea of deception equates much more closely to consciously controlling how situations appear to others.

The chapter ends with Sun Tzu introducing the idea that strategic analysis demands conscious calculation. To find the best customers and best sales situations, we must balance every sales opportunity's pros and cons.

This chapter provides the basic framework of Sun Tzu's strategy, and all these ideas are covered in more detail in later chapters.

Analysis

SUN TZU SAID:

This is war. 1

It is the most important skill in the nation.

It is the basis of life and death.

It is the philosophy of survival or destruction.

You must know it well.

6Your skill comes from five factors.

Study these factors when you plan war.

You must insist on knowing your situation.

1.	Discuss philosophy.
2.	Discuss the climate.
3.	Discuss the ground.
4.	Discuss leadership.
5.	Discuss military methods.

14It starts with your military philosophy.

Command your people in a way that gives them a higher shared purpose.

You can lead them to death.

You can lead them to life.

They must never fear danger or dishonesty.

Your Sales Position

1 This is selling.
It is the most valuable skill in any business.
It can bring you fortune or poverty.
It is your path to success or failure.
You must study sales seriously.

Five factors determine your skill.
Consider these factors when you analyze a sale.
You must know your strategic sales position:

1. Talk about your sales philosophy.
2. Talk about the changing trends.
3. Talk about your customers and prospects.
4. Talk about your sales talents.
5. And talk about your sales process.

Selling begins with your sales philosophy.
When you sell, you must always sell in a way that shares your customers' goals.
You will share your customers' failures.
You will share your customers' successes.
With this philosophy, you need not fear or lie to customers.

¹⁹Next, you have the climate.
It can be sunny or overcast.
It can be hot or cold.
It includes the timing of the seasons.

²³Next is the terrain.
It can be distant or near.
It can be difficult or easy.
It can be open or narrow.
It also determines your life or death.

²⁸Next is the commander.
He must be smart, trustworthy, caring, brave, and strict.

³⁰Finally, you have your military methods.
They include the shape of your organization.
This comes from your management philosophy.
You must master their use.

³⁴All five of these factors are critical.
As a commander, you must pay attention to them.
Understanding them brings victory.
Ignoring them means defeat.

Next are the changing trends.
Your attitude can be enthusiastic or negative.
Your product can be fashionable or stable.
All trends change over time.

Next are your customers and prospects.
They can be spread out or close by.
They can be resistant or eager.
Their minds can be open or closed.
Choosing the right market determines success or failure.

Next are your sales talents.
You must be smart, honest, caring, brave, and disciplined.

Finally, you need the right sales process.
This process depends on the organization to which you are selling.
You must always control the sales process.
You must understand your customers well.

All five of these factors are critical.
You must continuously analyze them.
You must understand them to be successful.
Ignore them and you will fail.

You must learn through planning. 2
You must question the situation.

³You must ask:
Which government has the right philosophy?
Which commander has the skill?
Which season and place has the advantage?
Which method of command works?
Which group of forces has the strength?
Which officers and men have the training?
Which rewards and punishments make sense?
This tells when you will win and when you will lose.
Some commanders perform this analysis.
If you use these commanders, you will win.
Keep them.
Some commanders ignore this analysis.
If you use these commanders, you will lose.
Get rid of them.

Plan an advantage by listening. 3
Adjust to the situations.
Get assistance from the outside.
Influence events.
Then planning can find opportunities and give you control.

2 Analysis reveals what is important in the sale.
You need to ask many questions.

You must ask:
Does your company offer a competitive product?
Do you have the sales skills you need?
Do you know the right time to sell to the customer?
Which sales process is right for the customer?
Which issues are important to the customer?
Do you know more than the competition?
Which sales are going to make you money?
The answers tell which sales you will win and which you will lose.
You must act on this type of analysis.
If you use it, you will be successful.
You will have a good sales career.
Too many salespeople ignore this analysis.
If you don't use it, your efforts will fail.
Your sales career will be short.

3 You discover your customers' interests by listening.
Listening gives you influence.
Listening makes it easy to win sales.
Listening is power.
Understand customers' desires and you can guide them.

Warfare is one thing. 4
It is a philosophy of deception.

[3]When you are ready, you try to appear incapacitated.
When active, you pretend inactivity.
When you are close to the enemy, you appear distant.
When far away, you pretend you are near.

[7]You can have an advantage and still entice an opponent.
You can be disorganized and still be decisive.
You can be ready and still be preparing.
You can be strong and still avoid battle.
You can be angry and still stop yourself.
You can humble yourself and still be confident.
You can be playing and still be working.
You can be close to an ally and still part ways.
You can attack a place without planning to do so.
You can leave a place without giving away your plan.

[17]You will find a place where you can win.
You cannot first signal your intentions.

4 Selling is one thing.
You must control your customers' perceptions.

If you have an advantage, you must seem humble.
When you are working hard, make it seem easy.
When problems seem large, you must make them seem small.
When advantages seem minor, you must make them appear large.

When you have an advantage, invite comparisons.
If you are caught off guard, appear confident.
When you are prepared, keep gathering information.
Even when your product is superior, avoid attacking competitors.
When you get upset, stop yourself from showing it.
You can appear modest even when you are confident.
You can have fun even when you are working hard.
You can like a sales partner but choose not to work with him or her.
You can close sales even when you didn't plan to do so.
You can give up on a proposal without giving up the sale.

You must find customers who need you.
Do not let them see how much you need them.

Manage to avoid battle until your organization can **5**
count on certain victory.
You must calculate many advantages.
Before you go to battle, your organization's analysis can indi-
cate that you may not win.
You can count few advantages.
Many advantages add up to victory.
Few advantages add up to defeat.
How can you know your advantages without analyzing them?
We can see where we are by means of our observations.
We can foresee our victory or defeat by planning.

5 Before investing in a sales process or closing a sale, you must know that the customer will buy your product.

The customer must have good reasons to buy.

Before wasting your time, you can see when you will not win the customer.

You can find too few reasons for customers to buy.

Having good reasons to buy wins you customers.

Having too few reasons to buy wastes your time.

How can you prioritize actions without analyzing them?

You can see where you are only by means of questioning.

You can foresee winning the sale or losing it by analysis.

Expense

Income

Chapter 2

作戰

Going to War: Choosing to Sell

Before you can really understand the implications of a career in sales, you must understand the economic demands of a highly competitive and emotionally demanding career. To be successful at selling, you must understand money. This reality fits extremely well with Sun Tzu's definition of victory as not simply winning battles but as making victory pay. This economic focus is one of the reasons that this strategy works so well in today's business world. If you want to succeed as a salesperson, you need to appreciate this chapter's economic lessons.

To begin, selling is expensive. Sun Tzu starts by discussing the economic demands of competition. Selling may pay well but only if you close sales. It is a risky profession even if you are on salary.

One of the biggest problems with commissioned sales is how uncertain the timing of its rewards is. This is the topic of the next section of this chapter. To address unpredictability, Sun Tzu advises minimizing spending rather than hoping things will go well.

Travel is often the biggest component of cost and, lest you think that this is the organization's problem, Sun Tzu explains why organizations that are unable to control costs are doomed.

Sun Tzu offers his strategy for dealing with costs: don't expect your company to pay for your service; expect your sales to pay for them. He calls this "feeding off the enemy."

In the chapter's final section, Sun Tzu says that your skill in making money is the only thing that makes a sales career possible.

Going to War

SUN TZU SAID:

Everything depends on your use of military philosophy. 1
Moving the army requires thousands of vehicles.
These vehicles must be loaded thousands of times.
The army must carry a huge supply of arms.
You need ten thousand acres of grain.
This results in internal and external shortages.
Any army consumes resources like an invader.
It uses up glue and paint for wood.
It requires armor for its vehicles.
People complain about the waste of a vast amount of metal.
It will set you back when you attempt to raise tens of thou-
sands of troops.

[12]Using a huge army makes war very expensive to win.
Long delays create a dull army and sharp defeats.
Attacking enemy cities drains your forces.
Long violent campaigns that exhaust the nation's resources
are wrong.

Choosing to Sell

1 Everything depends on your sales philosophy.
Traveling to see customers is expensive.
Building a territory takes time.
You want plenty of sales support from your company.
You want to be paid thousands of dollars in advances.
This results in a large investment from your company.
This drains resources from elsewhere in the company.
You want the best quality in sales resources.
You want others to support your efforts.
Others complain about how well salespeople are paid.
You take your time selling when you can depend on advances
against future sales.

Selling slowly is too costly to be successful.
A complacent salesperson always loses to a hungry one.
Long periods without a sale drain your enthusiasm.
Long sales cycles that deplete your time, energy, and resources are
wrong.

¹⁶Manage a dull army.
You will suffer sharp defeats.
You will drain your forces.
Your money will be used up.
Your rivals will multiply as your army collapses and they will
begin against you.
It doesn't matter how smart you are.
You cannot get ahead by taking losses!

²³You hear of people going to war too quickly.
Still, you won't see a skilled war that lasts a long time.

²⁵You can fight a war for a long time or you can make your
nation strong.
You can't do both.

Make no assumptions about all the dangers in using 2
military force.
Then you won't make assumptions about the benefits of
using arms either.

³You want to make good use of war.
Do not raise troops repeatedly.
Do not carry too many supplies.
Choose to be useful to your nation.
Feed off the enemy.
Make your army carry only the provisions it needs.

What happens when you are complacent?

You lose sales to someone who needs them more.

What happens when your enthusiasm fades?

You don't have the energy to continue.

As your sales efforts weaken, you inspire your competitors to attack you.

It doesn't matter how smart you think you are.

You can't get ahead once you've fallen behind.

You can sometimes move too fast in a sales process.

However, the longer the sales cycle, the more often you will fail.

You can try to move slowly when you are selling, or you can be successful.

You can't have it both ways.

2 You can never completely insure against failure when you go into sales.

You are therefore unlimited in the success that you can achieve from sales.

You want to make good use of your efforts.

Do not repeatedly ask for new prospects or territory.

Do not continually request more resources.

Support the needs of your company.

Quickly earn business from your customers.

Limit yourself to the resources you truly need.

The nation impoverishes itself shipping to troops that **3** are far away.

Distant transportation is costly for hundreds of families.

Buying goods with the army nearby is also expensive.

High prices also exhaust wealth.

If you exhaust your wealth, you then quickly hollow out your military.

Military forces consume a nation's wealth entirely.

War leaves households in the former heart of the nation with nothing.

[8]War destroys hundreds of families.

Out of every ten families, war leaves only seven.

War empties the government's storehouses.

Broken armies will get rid of their horses.

They will throw down their armor, helmets, and arrows.

They will lose their swords and shields.

They will leave their wagons without oxen.

War will consume 60 percent of everything you have.

Because of this, it is the intelligent commander's duty to **4** feed off the enemy.

[2]Use a cup of the enemy's food.

It is worth twenty of your own.

Win a bushel of the enemy's feed.

It is worth twenty of your own.

3 Selling to remote, new prospects is costly for you and your company.

Supporting distant customers puts more pressure on salespeople.

Conversely, selling to crowded, competitive markets is risky.

These high risks can also destroy your company.

When sales are slow, the company must accept orders of questionable value.

Lowering prices undermines your credibility entirely.

As a salesperson, cutting your prices to win a sale leaves you with nothing.

Undependable sales income puts pressure on your family.

Seven out of ten salespeople fail within the first few years.

Tough competition can consume your savings.

Failed salespeople must look for new employment.

They must give up the sales knowledge they have developed.

They lose their customers and contacts.

They give up their progress in building their territories.

Weak salespeople have to settle for smaller and smaller incomes.

4 Because of this, you must generate your income from sales to your existing prospects.

Win a dollar in commissions.

It is worth twenty in salary or advances.

Win a dollar in customer sales today.

It is worth twenty dollars of future potential.

[6]You can kill the enemy and frustrate him as well.
Take the enemy's strength from him by stealing away his
money.

[8]Fight for the enemy's supply wagons.
Capture his supplies by using overwhelming force.
Reward the first who capture them.
Then change their banners and flags.
Mix them in with your own wagons to increase your supply
line.
Keep your soldiers strong by providing for them.
This is what it means to beat the enemy while you grow
more powerful.

Make victory in war pay for itself. 5
Avoid expensive, long campaigns.
The military commander's knowledge is the key.
It determines whether the civilian officials can govern.
It determines whether the nation's households are peaceful
or a danger to the state.

Close sales aggressively.

You need to get the benefit of your customers' money as soon as possible.

Fight for customers' business.

Win sales by offering your customers persuasive benefits.

Reward those who buy first.

Use these first customers to bring in more customers.

Base your sales presentation on your past success with other customers.

Customer success is what makes you successful.

This is what is meant by helping the customer while you help yourself.

5 Make yourself successful by winning sales.
Don't make yourself poorer by lengthening sales cycles.

As a salesperson, your skill is the difference.

Quality salespeople make products and companies more appealing.

Your sales skill determines how easy or difficult it is to sell your product.

Uniting

Division

Focusing

Chapter 3

Planning an Attack: Planning Your Territory

If you are serious about a successful career in sales, this chapter offers invaluable lessons on focusing your efforts to build a territory. The central topic of this chapter is unity and focus and their effect on strength and power.

For Sun Tzu, unity and strength are not two separate ideas but a single idea, the concept of oneness. Oneness means both uniting with others and having a single purpose. This chapter's first lesson is that you must use the power of oneness at every level to successfully dominate your territory.

You cannot be passive in this process. To build a territory, you must attack it. In this chapter, Sun Tzu lists the basic forms of attack in descending order of effectiveness. The text warns against the worst of these: attacking a competitor's strongest positions.

Sun Tzu teaches an incremental approach to building your territory: fighting small, focused battles where you have the clear advantage. He explains how the relative size of your resources or relative product appeal determines your tactics in a given engagement.

Are you a salesperson or a politician? In its fourth section, the chapter warns against political thinking and explains how that thinking weakens your competitive strength.

Sun Tzu then details the five areas of knowledge that you must focus on to be successful.

The chapter ends by explaining how the test of your real knowledge is your overall effectiveness.

Planning an Attack

SUN TZU SAID:

Everyone relies on the arts of war. 1
A united nation is strong.
A divided nation is weak.
A united army is strong.
A divided army is weak.
A united force is strong.
A divided force is weak.
United men are strong.
Divided men are weak.
A united unit is strong.
A divided unit is weak.

[12]Unity works because it enables you to win every battle you
fight.
Still, this is the foolish goal of a weak leader.
Avoid battle and make the enemy's men surrender.
This is the right goal for a superior leader.

The best way to make war is to upset the enemy's plans. 2
The next best is to disrupt alliances.
The next best is to attack the opposing army.
The worst is to attack the enemy's cities.

Planning Your Territory

1 Everything depends on your selling skills.

A focused company is superior.

A diverse company is inferior.

A single product line is easy to sell.

Many different product lines are difficult to sell.

A concentrated effort is successful.

A divided effort fails.

A small territory is strong.

A spread-out territory is weak.

A unified message works well.

A mixed message works poorly.

You can meet a hundred objections and overcome them to win sales.

This doesn't make you a great salesperson.

You want to win sales without raising a single objection.

This is your highest goal.

2 It's best to sell before the prospect starts shopping.

The next best is to sell though referrals.

The next best is to show better value than the alternatives.

The worst is to attack a customer's past decisions.

⁵This is what happens when you attack a city.
You can attempt it, but you can't finish it.
First you must make siege engines.
You need the right equipment and machinery.
It takes three months and still you cannot win.
Then you try to encircle the area.
You use three more months without making progress.
Your command still doesn't succeed and this angers you.
You then try to swarm the city.
This kills a third of your officers and men.
You are still unable to draw the enemy out of the city.
This attack is a disaster.

Make good use of war. 3
Make the enemy's troops surrender.
You can do this fighting only minor battles.
You can draw their men out of their cities.
You can do it with small attacks.
You can destroy the men of a nation.
You must keep your campaign short.

⁸You must use total war, fighting with everything you have.
Never stop fighting when at war.
You can gain complete advantage.
To do this, you must plan your strategy of attack.

What happens when you try to change customers' minds?
You create resistance that works against you.
First, you must prepare arguments against their decisions.
You need to find leverage to change their thinking.
This can take months.
You must be persistent enough to turn them around.
After months of talking, most prospects will still not agree.
When you can't get agreement, you become frustrated.
You try to pressure customers into agreement.
You waste your limited time trying to persuade them.
The result is that you fail to win sales.
This type of selling is a disaster.

3 Make good use of your time.
You can win new customers.
You can do it without a single disagreement.
You can win customers away from their current suppliers.
You don't have to attack their past decisions directly.
You must focus your efforts on avoiding resistance.
You must find ways to win customers quickly.

In sales, you commit everything to winning customers.
Never stop selling when you are with prospects.
You can gain the advantage if you focus.
To do this, you must plan your sales strategy.

¹²The rules for making war are:
If you outnumber enemy forces ten to one, surround them.
If you outnumber them five to one, attack them.
If you outnumber them two to one, divide them.
If you are equal, then find an advantageous battle.
If you are fewer, defend against them.
If you are much weaker, evade them.

¹⁹Small forces are not powerful.
However, large forces cannot catch them.

You must master command. 4
The nation must support you.

³Supporting the military makes the nation powerful.
Not supporting the military makes the nation weak.

⁵The army's position is made more difficult by politicians in
three different ways.
Ignorant of the whole army's inability to advance, they order
an advance.
Ignorant of the whole army's inability to withdraw, they
order a withdrawal.
We call this tying up the army.
Politicians don't understand the army's business.
Still, they think they can run an army.
This confuses the army's officers.

The rules for winning customers are:

If your product is ten times better, just take orders.

If your product is five times better, assume the sale.

If your product is twice as good, pick better prospects.

If your product is equal, sell only to the best prospects.

If your product is weaker, sell where the competition cannot.

If your product is much weaker, find market niches.

Small companies cannot sell to broad markets.

However, large companies cannot satisfy niche markets.

4 As a salesperson, you control your territory.

Your territory must support you.

You are strong when your territory is well managed.

Your position is weak when your territory is poorly managed.

Poor territory management creates problems for salespeople in three ways.

Ignorant of which prospects are the best, you try to contact everyone.

Ignorant of which prospects are bad, you are discouraged from selling to anyone.

You tie yourself up in knots.

Ignorant of management, you want different prospects.

You think you are in the wrong market.

This undermines the effectiveness of your efforts.

¹²Politicians don't know the army's chain of command.
They give the army too much freedom.
This will create distrust among the army's officers.

¹⁵The entire army becomes confused and distrusting.
This invites invasion by many different rivals.
We say correctly that disorder in an army kills victory.

You must know five things to win: 5
Victory comes from knowing when to attack and when to
avoid battle.
Victory comes from correctly using both large and small
forces.
Victory comes from everyone sharing the same goals.
Victory comes from finding opportunities in problems.
Victory comes from having a capable commander and the
government leaving him alone.
You must know these five things.
You then know the theory of victory.

We say: 6
"Know yourself and know your enemy.
You will be safe in every battle.
You may know yourself but not know the enemy.
You will then lose one battle for every one you win.
You may not know yourself or the enemy.
You will then lose every battle."

♦ ♦ ♦

You must understand your priorities in selling.

You cannot sell whenever and to whomever you want.

This creates weak customer relationships.

Unfocused selling confuses your prospects and creates distrust.

This invites the competition to win away your customers.

A unfocused sales process destroys your chances of success.

5 You must know five things to win customers.

You must know which prospects to sell to and which prospects to avoid.

You must know when to sell a big order and when to sell a small order.

You must know how to share your customers' goals.

You must know how to turn problems into opportunities.

You must know when to work your customers and when to leave them alone.

Master these five categories of knowledge.

You then know the philosophy of winning sales.

6 Pay attention.

Know your products and your prospects.

If you do, you can win sales in any situation.

You may know your products but not your prospects.

Then, for every sale you make, you will lose another.

You may know neither your products nor your prospects.

Then you will lose every sale.

✦ ✦ ✦

Siege

Positioning

Focusing

Chapter 4

Positioning: Sales Process

Sales strategy means finding ways to advance your position with customers rather than fighting the competition. Sun Tzu's concept of positioning means moving to a new position *only* when an opportunity presents itself. As a salesperson, you can use this process directly to create a unique selling proposition—a sales position—for you, your company, and your product.

Sun Tzu starts by explaining that you must take your cues from your customers in the sales process. You control the sales process, but they control its timing.

In the second section, the text explains that your success first depends on your ability to defend your current position or keep the sales process going when you cannot close it.

The third section explains that after you see an opportunity, you must be able use it easily and effortlessly. This requires your ability to adjust your sales position to the opportunity and leverage than new position to close the sale.

In the fourth section, Sun Tzu provides a simple formula for calculating whether or not you can succeed in winning a new position or a given sale; this is done by calculating your relative strength at the place and time of decision.

In the final section, Sun Tzu briefly explains how good positioning leads to confidence. Your confidence is critical in getting agreement from your customers.

Positioning

Sun Tzu said:

Learn from the history of successful battles. 1
First, you should control the situation not try to win.
If you adjust to the enemy, you will find a way to win.
The opportunity to win does not come from you.
The opportunity to win comes from your enemy.

6You must pick good battles.
You can control them until you can win.
You cannot win them until the enemy enables your victory.

9We say:
You see the opportunity for victory; you don't control it.

Sales Process

1 Learn from your past successes.
Your first actions should guide the sales process, not win the sale.
As you adjust to your prospect, you will find a way to win the sale.
The opportunity to win doesn't come from your needs.
The opportunity to win comes from the needs of your prospect.

You must pick good prospects.
You can guide these prospects until you can win their business.
You cannot close the sale until the prospect enables your success.

Pay attention:
You must see the opportunity to close; you can't create it.

You are sometimes unable to win. 2
You must then defend.
You will eventually be able to win.
You must then attack.
Defend when you have insufficient strength.
Attack when you have a surplus of strength.

7You must defend yourself well.
Save your forces and dig in.
You must attack well.
Move your forces when you have a clear advantage.

11You must always protect yourself until you can completely
triumph.

Some may see how to win. 3
However, they cannot move their forces where they must.
This demonstrates limited ability.

4Some can struggle to a victory and the whole world may
praise their winning.
This also demonstrates a limited ability.

6Win as easily as picking up a fallen hair.
Don't use all of your forces.
See the time to move.
Don't try to find something clever.
Hear the clap of thunder.
Don't try to hear something subtle.

2 You are not always positioned to win a sale.
Therefore, you must keep the sales process going.
You will eventually be in a position to win the sale.
Then you must ask for the order.
Stay in the sale when you are not in a position to close it.
Close the sale when you are certain you will win it.

You must nurture the sale carefully.
Say little and learn about the customer's business.
You must close sales decisively.
Demand customer action when the benefits are clear.

Keep yourself in contention for the sale until you are certain to win it.

3 You may see what customers need.
Yet you fail to position your product so that you meet those needs.
This shows a limited ability.

You may win a difficult sale that requires a great deal of effort and everyone will praise you.
This also shows a limited ability.

Good sales are effortless.
Avoid using all your resources.
Vision is seeing what is obvious.
Don't try to find something hidden.
Hearing the customer is easy if you listen.
Don't imagine what you want to hear.

[12]Learn from the history of successful battles.
Victory goes to those who make winning easy.
A good battle is one that you will obviously win.
It doesn't take intelligence to win a reputation.
It doesn't take courage to achieve success.

[17]You must win your battles without effort.
Avoid difficult struggles.
Fight when your position must win.
You always win by preventing your defeat.

[21]You must engage only in winning battles.
Position yourself where you cannot lose.
Never waste an opportunity to defeat your enemy.

[24]You win a war by first assuring yourself of victory.
Only afterward do you look for a fight.
Outmaneuver the enemy before the first battle and then
fight to win.

Learn from your successful efforts.

Winning sales requires making the job easy.

A good sale is one that you simply assume you will win.

You are foolish if you want to make a name for yourself.

Avoid conflict if you want to have real success in selling.

You want to win sales without fighting your prospects.

Avoid sales battles.

Close sales when you are certain you will win.

Sell to customers who have already sold themselves.

You must sell only to customers that you can win.

Position yourself where you cannot lose the sale.

Await your opportunity and then ask for the order.

You must first know that the prospect needs your product.

Only then do you ask the prospect to decide.

You should never demand a decision before you are certain you will win the sale.

You must make good use of war. 4
Study military philosophy and the art of defense.
You can control your victory or defeat.

4This is the art of war:
"1.   Discuss the distances.
2.   Discuss your numbers.
3.   Discuss your calculations.
4.   Discuss your decisions.
5.   Discuss victory.

10The ground determines the distance.
The distance determines your numbers.
Your numbers determine your calculations.
Your calculations determine your decisions.
Your decisions determine your victory."

15Creating a winning war is like balancing a coin of gold
against a coin of silver.
Creating a losing war is like balancing a coin of silver
against a coin of gold.

Winning a battle is always a matter of people. 5
You pour them into battle like a flood of water pouring into
a deep gorge.
This is a matter of positioning.

♦ ♦ ♦

4 You must make good use of your time.
Examine your situation objectively.
Your discipline determines your success or failure.

The sales process requires:
1.   a discussion of customer qualifications,
2.   a discussion of customer needs,
3.   a discussion of product value,
4.   a discussion of your proposal,
5.   and a discussion finalizing the sale.

Customers determine their qualifications.
Their qualifications determine their needs.
Their needs determine the value of the product.
Product value determines your proposal.
Your proposal determines how the sale is finalized.

You win sales when customers know that they are getting more
than they are giving.
You will lose sales if they feel that they are giving more than they
are getting.

5 You must be completely confident when you close a sale.
The weight of benefits to the customer must be obvious and over-
whelming.
This is the matter of your sales position.

✦ ✦ ✦

Standards

Standards

Momentum

Surprise

Surprise

Chapter 5

Momentum: Persuasion

In the world of sales, Sun Tzu's concept of momentum provides a powerful tool of persuasion. However, Sun Tzu defines momentum in a very specific way. To create momentum as a force for change, you must alternate between well-accepted ideas that the customer is comfortable with and ideas that are novel and surprising. This combination of the well established and the creative creates a sense of progress.

In the chapter's first section, Sun Tzu explains that every type of sales is the same, combining actions that are either expected or surprising.

The second section explains that predictability and surprise depend on one another. To impress customers with new viewpoints, you must first prepare them using ideas with which they are comfortable. There are an infinite number of creative ideas, but unless they are built on familiar concepts, they seem outlandish.

Sun Tzu uses the third section to show us how the persuasive use of momentum creates tension. Closing the sale is a matter of having the right timing to release the tension created by your use of persuasion.

The fourth section addresses the fact that although you never know exactly what is going on in the customer's mind, you can use the persuasion of momentum to control it.

In the final section, the pressure of momentum is explained in terms of its effect upon your customer's thinking.

Momentum

You control a large group the same as you control a few. 1
You just divide their ranks correctly.
You fight a large army the same as you fight a small one.
You only need the right position and communication.
You may meet a large enemy army.
You must be able to sustain an enemy attack without being
defeated.
You must correctly use both surprise and direct action.
Your army's position must increase your strength.
Troops flanking an enemy can smash them like eggs.
You must correctly use both strength and weakness.

It is the same in all battles. 2
You use a direct approach to engage the enemy.
You use surprise to win.

4You must use surprise for a successful invasion.
Surprise is as infinite as the weather and land.
Surprise is as inexhaustible as the flow of a river.

66   The Art of War 5: Momentum

Persuasion

1 Complex sales are the same as simple ones.
You only need to divide your time among more people.
Sales to large companies are the same as sales to small ones.
You need to understand their organization.
You may meet larger competitors.
You can compete against them and you should never lose a sale to them.
You only need to use creative and standard methods.
Together, they increase your influence with a prospect.
You must attack competitors on their weaknesses.
You must understand both their strengths and weaknesses.

2 In selling, you must use standard approaches in making contact with a prospect.
Your creativity wins the sale.

You must use creativity to be successful in all sales.
Creativity uses the unique conditions of the situation.
No sale is ever exactly the same as another.

7You can be stopped and yet recover the initiative.
You must use your days and months correctly.

9If you are defeated, you can recover.
You must use the four seasons correctly.

11There are only a few notes in the scale.
Yet you can always rearrange them.
You can never hear every song of victory.

14There are only a few basic colors.
Yet you can always mix them.
You can never see all the shades of victory.

17There are only a few flavors.
Yet you can always blend them.
You can never taste all the flavors of victory.

20You fight with momentum.
There are only a few types of surprises and direct actions.
Yet you can always vary the ones you use.
There is no limit to the ways you can win.

24Surprise and direct action give birth to each other.
They are like a circle without end.
You cannot exhaust all their possible combinations!

Surging water flows together rapidly. 3
Its pressure washes away boulders.
This is momentum.

If you are creative, you can be rejected and yet return.
Yesterday's failure becomes tomorrow's new approach.

If you are creative, you can lose a sale and still recover.
You can lose one season and come back the next.

There are only a few basic sales techniques.
Yet you can combine them in any number of ways.
You can always find a better way to sell.

There are only a few basic human needs.
Yet every person feels them differently.
You must always find your prospect's unique perspective.

There are only a few kinds of value.
Yet they change from person to person, moment to moment.
You can discover new benefits from customers.

You win sales with persuasion.
You use only a few creative and standard techniques.
Yet you can combine them to make each process unique.
You have no limit to the ways you can win.

Creative and standard approaches require each other.
You must use both and move from one to the other.
If you use both, no one can stop you.

3 Creativity gives impact to ideas.
The force of your ideas can wash away resistance.
This is persuasion.

⁴A hawk suddenly strikes a bird.
Its contact alone kills the prey.
This is timing.

⁷You must fight only winning battles.
Your momentum must be overwhelming.
Your timing must be exact.

¹⁰Your momentum is like the tension of a bent crossbow.
Your timing is like the pulling of a trigger.

War is very complicated and confusing. 4
Battle is chaotic.
Nevertheless, you must not allow chaos.

⁴War is very sloppy and messy.
Positions turn around.
Nevertheless, you must never be defeated.

⁷Chaos gives birth to control.
Fear gives birth to courage.
Weakness gives birth to strength.

¹⁰You must control chaos.
This depends on your planning.
Your men must brave their fears.
This depends on their momentum.

¹⁴You have strengths and weaknesses.
These come from your position.

You close the sale with good timing.
Asking for the order at the right time overcomes resistance.
This is closing.

Success in sales depends on your skill.
Your creativity must be persuasive.
You must time your closing exactly.

Persuasion should increase the tension in the sale.
Closing should release that tension in a moment.

4 Sales are always complicated and confusing.
Selling is messy.
It is your job to put order into the process.

Your position in the sale is never clear.
It is constantly changing.
Nevertheless, you must never lose the sale.

Your customer's confusion requires your clarity.
Your customer's uncertainty requires your confidence.
Your customer's weakness requires your strength.

You must clarify what is confusing.
This depends on your analysis.
You must overcome uncertainty.
This depends on your persuasiveness.

You have both strengths and weaknesses.
They arise from your position.

¹⁶You must force the enemy to move to your advantage.

Use your position.

The enemy must follow you.

Surrender a position.

The enemy must take it.

You can offer an advantage to move him.

You can use your men to move him.

You can use your strength to hold him.

You want a successful battle. 5

To do this, you must seek momentum.

Do not just demand a good fight from your people.

You must pick good people and then give them momentum.

⁵You must create momentum.

You create it with your men during battle.

This is comparable to rolling trees and stones.

Trees and stones roll because of their shape and weight.

Offer men safety and they will stay calm.

Endanger them and they will act.

Give them a place and they will hold.

Round them up and they will march.

¹³You make your men powerful in battle with momentum.

This should be like rolling round stones down over a high,

steep cliff.

Momentum is critical.

You must always take the lead in moving the sale forward.
Offer different types of proposals.
Your customers must think about them.
Offer customers something without risk.
They will want to take it.
You can use promotional offers to move them.
You can use your ideas to motivate them.
You can use your certainty to prevent a bad decision.

5 You must create the perfect situation for closing the sale.
You work toward it by building your influence.
You do not demand the sale from the customer.
You offer a great proposal and then you use real persuasion.

You must keep the sale moving forward.
You do this by keeping the prospect engaged.
One task must naturally lead to another.
The process must keep prospects moving.
Satisfaction with the status quo keeps them from acting.
Problems force them to act.
Solid information gets their attention.
Surround customers with information and they must act.

You make yourself powerful in a sale with persuasion.
You want everything moving inevitably toward a decision in your
favor.
Use persuasion.

Division

Chapter 6

Weakness and Strength: Disadvantages and Advantages

As a salesperson, you can use the techniques in this chapter to create an advantage for yourself while putting your opposition at a disadvantage. Weakness is both what your customers need and what your competitors overlook. Your strength comes from their weaknesses.

In the first section, Sun Tzu begins to clarify this complex idea by explaining that if you get to the customer first, you are naturally stronger than if you get to the customer after competitors do.

The second section continues this idea by explaining that you can make progress more quickly by going into areas that are overlooked by your competitors.

In the third section, Sun Tzu then explains the need to keep your movement and proposals secret while you learn about the secrets of customers and competitors.

The fourth section teaches you to focus on the areas where the lack of competition has given you strength.

In the fifth section, the lesson is that by when you use focus and keep your focus a secret from competitors, your customers cannot resist you and competitors cannot counter you.

Sun Tzu summarizes weakness and strength in the sixth section by applying these ideas to planning, action, position, and meeting competitive challenges.

In the final two sections, the text explains how using weakness requires remaining flexible and using the path of least resistance.

Weakness and Strength

SUN TZU SAID:

Always arrive first to the empty battlefield to await the 1
enemy at your leisure.
After the battleground is occupied and you hurry to it, fighting is more difficult.

3You want a successful battle.
Move your men, but not into opposing forces.

5You can make the enemy come to you.
Offer him an advantage.
You can make the enemy avoid coming to you.
Threaten him with danger.

9When the enemy is fresh, you can tire him.
When he is well fed, you can starve him.
When he is relaxed, you can move him.

Disadvantages and Advantages

1 You want the advantage of getting to the customer before the competition does.
Avoid selling to prospects where the competition is already entrenched.

Your only goal is to win sales.
Use your time; don't waste it on the competition.

You can make customers come to you.
You must entice them with unique benefits.
You can stop competitors from attacking you.
Make it clear that they are wasting their time.

If prospects are comfortable, make them uncomfortable.
If prospects are satisfied, make them hungry for more.
If prospects are lethargic, ask them to do something.

Leave any place without haste. 2
Hurry to where you are unexpected.
You can easily march hundreds of miles without tiring.
To do so, travel through areas that are deserted.
You must take whatever you attack.
Attack when there is no defense.
You must have walls to defend.
Defend where it is impossible to attack.

9Be skilled in attacking.
Give the enemy no idea where to defend.

11Be skillful in your defense.
Give the enemy no idea where to attack.

Be subtle! Be subtle! 3
Arrive without any clear formation.
Ghostly! Ghostly!
Arrive without a sound.
You must use all your skill to control the enemy's decisions.

6Advance where he can't defend.
Charge through his openings.
Withdraw where the enemy cannot chase you.
Move quickly so that he cannot catch you.

2 Abandon an established position slowly.
Quickly stake out markets before the competition does.
You can make easy progress in any sale.
To do so, you must uncover unexplored possibilities.
You must be certain to close every sale you go after.
You do this by going after prospects who need you.
You must always keep customers that you have won.
You must leave no needs for your competition to satisfy.

You must be skilled in winning customers.
Fill needs that the competition overlooks.

You must be skilled in keeping customers.
Leave no unmet needs for the competition to exploit.

3 You must be clever about your intentions.
Don't let customers assume they know what you offer.
You must be secretive about your proposals.
Don't let competitors know with whom you are working.
You must use your skill to control customers' thinking.

Make sales progress where customers can't resist you.
Attack the areas where they need help.
Quickly withdraw any ideas that create a conflict.
Change your position so the customer can't fight you.

[10]Always pick your own battles.
The enemy can hide behind high walls and deep trenches.
Do not try to win by fighting him directly.
Instead, attack a place that he must recapture.
Avoid the battles that you don't want.
You can divide the ground and yet defend it.
Don't give the enemy anything to win.
Divert him by coming to where you defend.

Make other men take a position while you take none. 4
Then focus your forces where the enemy divides his forces.
Where you focus, you unite your forces.
When the enemy divides, he creates many small groups.
You want your large group to attack one of his small ones.
Then you have many men where the enemy has but a few.
Your larger force can overwhelm his smaller one.
Then go on to the next small enemy group.
You can take them one at a time.

You must keep the place that you have chosen as a 5
battleground a secret.
The enemy must not know.
Force the enemy to prepare his defense in many places.
You want the enemy to defend many places.
Then you can choose where to fight.
His forces will be weak there.

You must pick your sales situations.

Customers can be secretive and protective.

You must not propose your product directly.

Instead, discover customers' goals and address them.

You must avoid sales conflicts.

You can defend your customers from any competitor.

Don't leave the competition any needs to satisfy.

Divert competitors from coming after your accounts.

4 Learn customers' positions and keep yourself flexible.

Identify a few key areas where customers have needs.

When you focus, you become more powerful.

When customers divide their attention, they create needs.

You must focus all your attention on their needs.

Spend your time where customers have not spent theirs.

Use your knowledge to overcome their lack of information.

You must offer one small idea at a time to help them.

You must lead them one step at a time.

5 You must keep your prospects, your plans, and your proposals a secret.

Your competitors must not know them.

Force them to defend against every possible argument.

They will spread themselves too thin.

You can choose the key issues to fight them on.

They are unable to prepare in those areas.

7If he reinforces his front lines, he depletes his rear.
If he reinforces his rear, he depletes his front.
If he reinforces his right flank, he depletes his left.
If he reinforces his left flank, he depletes his right.
Without knowing the place of attack, he cannot prepare.
Without knowing the right place, he will be weak everywhere.

13The enemy has weak points.
Prepare your men against them.
He has strong points.
Make his men prepare themselves against you.

You must know the battleground. 6
You must know the time of battle.
You can then travel a thousand miles and still win the battle.

4The enemy should not know the battleground.
He shouldn't know the time of battle.
His left flank will be unable to support his right.
His right will be unable to support his left.
His front lines will be unable to support his rear.
His rear will be unable to support his front.
His support is distant even if it is only ten miles away.
What unknown place can be close?

12You control the balance of forces.
The enemy may have many men but they are superfluous.
How can they help him to victory?

If they focus on price, they hurt their claims of best quality.
If they focus on quality, they hurt their claims of low prices.
If they focus on quickness, they weaken claims of accuracy.
If they focus on accuracy, they weaken claims of quickness.
Without knowing your issue, they cannot fight you directly.
If they claim every advantage, they are weak everywhere.

Customers have needs.
You must prepare to address them.
Competitors have strengths.
Make them try to attack you on your strengths.

6 You must know the customer's key issues.
You must know when the customer needs to buy.
You can then win the sale despite strong competition.

Your competitors may not know the key issues.
They should never know when you are asking for the sale.
Let them sell inappropriate ideas as well as good ones.
The inappropriate ones discredit their good ideas.
Let them sell useless features as well as valuable ones.
The useless features raise the cost of their valuable ones.
You can let them claim that they have a good product.
They can still miss the customer's needs.

You can influence the sense of value in the sale.
Your competitor can have too many features.
Are they valuable if the customer doesn't need them?

¹⁵We say:
You must let victory happen.

¹⁷The enemy may have many men.
You can still control him without a fight.

When you form your strategy, know the strengths and 7
weaknesses of your plan.
When you execute a plan, know how to manage both action
and inaction.
When you take a position, know the deadly and the winning
grounds.
When you enter into battle, know when you have too many
or too few men.

⁵Use your position as your war's centerpiece.
Arrive at the battle without a formation.
Don't take a position in advance.
Then even the best spies can't report it.
Even the wisest general cannot plan to counter you.
Take a position where you can triumph using superior numbers.
Keep opposing forces ignorant.
Everyone should learn your location after your position has
given you success.
No one should know how your location gives you a winning
position.
Make a successful battle one from which the enemy cannot
recover.
You must continually adjust your position to his position.

Pay attention:
You must let yourself win the sale.

The competition may have many more resources.
You can still control it without a direct battle.

7 When you plan, know your customers' strengths and weaknesses.
In meetings, know when you need to persuade and when you need to listen.
When you take a position, know what is important to customers and what isn't.
When you sell, know if you are addressing too many or too few of their needs.

The best policy for any salesperson is to remain flexible.
Don't go into a sale with a standard product offering.
Avoid initial proposals.
Then competitors cannot discredit your proposal.
You can beat them if they don't know what to expect.
Take a position when you see an opportunity to use your influence.
Keep your competitors in the dark.
Their salespeople may learn about your proposal when it has already been accepted.
They should never know why your proposal is so pleasing to the customer.
Make sure your proposal is one that they cannot easily improve upon.
You must adapt proposals to the key issues of the customer.

Manage your military position like water. 8
Water takes every shape.
It avoids the high and moves to the low.
Your war can take any shape.
It must avoid the strong and strike the weak.
Water follows the shape of the land that directs its flow.
Your forces follow the enemy, who determines how you win.

[8]Make war without a standard approach.
Water has no consistent shape.
If you follow the enemy's shifts and changes, you can always
find a way to win.
We call this shadowing.

[12]Fight five different campaigns without a firm rule for victory.
Use all four seasons without a consistent position.
Your timing must be sudden.
A few weeks determine your failure or success.

✦ ✦ ✦

8 You must remain flexible in the sales process.
Like water, you can take any shape.
Water naturally moves from the high and flows to the low.
You can adjust to any situation.
You must avoid strength and attack weakness.
Water follows the shape of the land that directs its flow.
You follow your customers' needs to create your offer.

You must avoid a rigid sales presentation.
Water has no consistent shape.
You win sales by following customers and continually adapting to their needs.
Act on their signals.

Use different tactics; no single approach always wins.
No specific timing and no single proposal are always right.
You must always create a sense of urgency.
An instant may determine your success or failure.

Chapter 7

Armed Conflict: Sales Contact

For the salesperson, this chapter serves as an outline for handling the sensitive task of making sales contact with customers. In this chapter, Sun Tzu warns against engaging in direct confrontations without a decisive advantage. The later part of the chapter covers techniques for succeeding in these confrontations when they occur.

A salesperson must be sensitive to the fact that people don't like being sold to. The first section of this chapter explains the dangers of conflict and that it cannot be undertaken carelessly.

Salespeople must avoid chasing after their customers. The second section explains the disasters that occur when you rush to engage an opponent without preparation.

You manage the sales process by going through a series of steps. The third section reemphasizes the need for deception—that is, controlling others' perceptions—in such confrontations.

Most salespeople like to hear themselves speak, but customers don't enjoy it nearly as much. Sun Tzu discusses the need for improved methods of communication during these situations. Good communication is the primary key to winning contact.

The fifth part of this chapter addresses the proper timing for making contact in order to control people's emotions.

When you are selling, the last thing you want to do is create resistance. In the final section, Sun Tzu provides a short but critical list of rules for avoiding mistakes during contact with the enemy.

Armed Conflict

SUN TZU SAID:

Everyone uses the arts of war. 1
You accept orders from the government.
Then you assemble your army.
You organize your men and build camps.
You must avoid disasters from armed conflict.

6Seeking armed conflict can be disastrous.
Because of this, a detour can be the shortest path.
Because of this, problems can become opportunities.

9Use an indirect route as your highway.
Use the search for advantage to guide you.
When you fall behind, you must catch up.
When you get ahead, you must wait.
You must know the detour that most directly accomplishes
your plan.

14Undertake armed conflict when you have an advantage.
Seeking armed conflict for its own sake is dangerous.

Sales Contact

1 Everyone uses the art of sales.
You accept your assignment from the company.
You assemble your leads and prospects.
You happily organize and build them into a territory.
However, the most difficult job is sales contact.

Sales contact is uncomfortable for everyone.
You cannot plan the path it will take.
You must expect problems and turn them into opportunities.

You must plan to take an indirect route to your goal.
You must plan to entice customers with benefits.
When you stumble, you must know how to catch up.
When you get ahead of the customer, you must slow down.
You must know how to plan to overcome objections that delay
acceptance.

You alone can make the sales contact successful.
All customer contact is inherently difficult.

You can build up an army to fight for an advantage. 2
Then you won't catch the enemy.
You can force your army to go fight for an advantage.
Then you abandon your heavy supply wagons.

⁵You keep only your armor and hurry after the enemy.
You avoid stopping day or night.
You use many roads at the same time.
You go hundreds of miles to fight for an advantage.
Then the enemy catches your commanders and your army.
Your strong soldiers get there first.
Your weaker soldiers follow behind.
Using this approach, only one in ten will arrive.
You can try to go fifty miles to fight for an advantage.
Then your commanders and army will stumble.
Using this method, only half of your soldiers will make it.
You can try to go thirty miles to fight for an advantage.
Then only two out of three will get there.

¹⁸If you make your army travel without good supply lines,
your army will die.
Without supplies and food, your army will die.
If you don't save the harvest, your army will die.

2 You can offer many arguments about product benefits.
You will then lose the customer.
You can rush through the sales process proposing benefits.
You then fail to learn about the customer.

You can defend your product and ask directly for the order.
You can work day and night.
You can work with many different customer contacts.
You can spend all your time preaching product benefits.
The customer can still reject your product and company.
You think you are winning the sale at first.
Over time your weaknesses will show.
Only a small fraction of your effort is useful.
You can try shortcuts in the sales process.
Your proposals will still fall short.
You are wasting half your time.
You can rush sales that are almost complete.
You may win two out of three.

If you try to eliminate needed steps in the sales process, it will cost you sales.
Without the proper information, you lose sales.
Without the proper groundwork, you lose sales.

²¹Do not let any of your potential enemies know what you
are planning.
Still, you must not hesitate to form alliances.
You must know the mountains and forests.
You must know where the obstructions are.
You must know where the marshes are.
If you don't, you cannot move the army.
If you don't, you must use local guides.
If you don't, you can't take advantage of the terrain.

You make war by making a false stand. 3
By finding an advantage, you can move.
By dividing and joining, you can reinvent yourself and
transform the situation.
You can move as quickly as the wind.
You can rise like the forest.
You can invade and plunder like fire.
You can stay as motionless as a mountain.
You can be as mysterious as the fog.
You can strike like sounding thunder.

¹⁰Divide your troops to plunder the villages.
When on open ground, dividing is an advantage.
Don't worry about organization; just move.
Be the first to find a new route that leads directly to a win-
ning plan.
This is how you are successful at armed conflict.

Instead, you must initially keep quiet about what you are planning to sell.

You must meet with people and talk with them.

You must know the customer's business.

You must know where the customer's problems are.

You must avoid getting bogged down in politics.

You must be knowledgeable to make the sale.

You must rely on your contacts in the business.

You must take advantage of the customer's thinking.

3 You must disguise your desire to make a sale.

By uncovering the customer's needs, you can make progress.

By tailoring your sales presentation, you can reposition your product and transform your offering.

To make sales, you must think on your feet.

You must eventually stand up and make your point.

You must be aggressive and hungry.

You must be quiet and patient.

You must keep your plans to yourself.

You must be bold and courageous.

When managing your territory, prioritize your activities.

When an opportunity offers itself, come to an agreement.

Don't think about it; just act.

Find better ways to help customers make their businesses successful.

This is how you are successful at customer contact.

Military experience says: 4
"You can speak, but you will not be heard.
You must use gongs and drums.
You cannot really see your forces just by looking.
You must use banners and flags."

6You must master gongs, drums, banners, and flags.
Place people as a single unit where they can all see and hear.
You must unite them as one.
Then the brave cannot advance alone.
The fearful cannot withdraw alone.
You must force them to act as a group.

12In night battles, you must use numerous fires and drums.
In day battles, you must use many banners and flags.
You must position your people to control what they see and
hear.

You control your army by controlling its morale. 5
As a general, you must be able to control emotions.

3In the morning, a person's energy is high.
During the day, it fades.
By evening, a person's thoughts turn to home.
You must use your troops wisely.
Avoid the enemy's high spirits.
Strike when his men are lazy and want to go home.
This is how you master energy.

4 Experience in sales teaches us:
"Words alone are not enough.
 Use pictures and charts.
 Demonstrating is not enough.
 Use showmanship and magic."

Use pictures, props, and showmanship to get everyone's attention.
Position your products simply so everyone can see their value.
Tie your arguments together.
Don't offer innovative ideas alone.
Tie them to comfortable, familiar ideas.
Every idea must amplify a single, clear message.

When you are unknown, you must create excitement and interest.
If you are better known, you still must keep your line interesting.
You must take a position that everyone can understand and appreciate.

5 You must get your customers' attention.
As a salesperson, you must use emotion.

In the morning, customer resistance is high.
During the day, it fades.
By evening, customers want to go home.
You must use your time wisely.
Avoid tough resistance.
Close when resistance fades and customers want to go home.
This is how you master energy.

¹⁰Use discipline to await the chaos of battle.
Keep relaxed to await a crisis.
This is how you master emotion.

¹³Stay close to home to await a distant enemy.
Stay comfortable to await the weary enemy.
Stay well fed to await the hungry enemy.
This is how you master power.

Don't entice the enemy when his ranks are orderly. 6
You must not attack when his formations are solid.
This is how you master adaptation.

⁴You must follow these military rules.
Do not take a position facing the high ground.
Do not oppose those with their backs to the wall.
Do not follow those who pretend to flee.
Do not attack the enemy's strongest men.
Do not swallow the enemy's bait.
Do not block an army that is heading home.
Leave an escape outlet for a surrounded army.
Do not press a desperate foe.
This is how you use military skills.

Keep organized when the customer is confused.
Stay quiet while the customer blows off steam.
This is how you master your feelings.

Stick to your point and wait for others to respond.
Stay friendly as you wear down the customer's resistance.
You will be successful if you serve the needs of others.
This is how you master persuasion.

6 Do not create organized resistance.
Do not attack firmly held beliefs.
This is how you master adaptation.

You must follow these sales rules.
Do not take a position against strong feelings.
Do not fight an argument based on a lack of alternatives.
Do not accept those who only pretend to agree.
Do not attack the strongest competition against you.
Do not believe everything the customer tells you.
Do not argue with a customer who agrees with you.
Give the customer an agreeable alternative.
Do not press the customer too hard for a decision.
These are the rules of selling.

Knowing   Foreseeing

Foreknowing   Knowing

Chapter 8

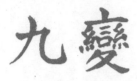 

Adaptability: Adjusting to the Situation

Salespeople must continually address new obstacles that arise in the sales process. The topic of this chapter is the need to continually change your plans based upon changing conditions. In Sun Tzu's view, successful strategies must be dynamic.

Selling requires surmounting certain specific challenges. In the chapter's first section, Sun Tzu lists situations (covered in greater detail in several other chapters) that show the need to constantly change your plans.

What looks like a sales objection is often the source of a sales advantage. The next short section makes the point that you can be creative and constantly adapt your methods without being inconsistent in your results.

You should know your own weaknesses in sales, but you must adjust to the weaknesses of your competitors and the needs of your customers to sell successfully. The third section, also short, explains that you can use the dynamics of competitive situations to control the behavior of others.

It is the customer's job to come up with objections. In the fourth section, Sun Tzu covers the need to address the unpredictability of opponents in planning the defense of your position.

All sales people have weaknesses. In the final section, Sun Tzu lists the five weaknesses of leaders and explains how you can defend against them in yourself and use them in others.

Adaptability

Sun Tzu said:

Everyone uses the arts of war. 1
As a general, you get your orders from the government.
You gather your troops.
On dangerous ground, you must not camp.
Where the roads intersect, you must join your allies.
When an area is cut off, you must not delay in it.
When you are surrounded, you must scheme.
In a life-or-death situation, you must fight.
There are roads that you must not take.
There are armies that you must not fight.
There are strongholds that you must not attack.
There are positions that you must not defend.
There are government commands that must not be obeyed.

[14]Military leaders must be experts in knowing how to adapt
to find an advantage.
This will teach you the use of war.

[16]Some commanders are not open to making adjustments to
find an advantage.
They can know the shape of the terrain.
Still, they cannot find an advantageous position.

Adjusting to the Situation

1 There are basic rules in selling.
You get your territory from the company.
You organize your sales process.
When the sale is impossible, you must not waste your time.
When you share goals, you must make partners.
When you are rejected, you must not give up.
When you are outmaneuvered, you must get creative.
When you are in a do-or-die situation, you must win.
There are products and services you should not sell.
There are customers you don't want.
There are competitors you cannot challenge.
There are proposals you must not defend.
There are times when you ignore standard company policy.

You must work to become an expert at knowing how to adapt to win a sale.
Adapting to the situation is the key to success.

Some salespeople are not open to changing their positions to fit a given situation.
They might know what the customer thinks.
Still, they are unable to identify their opportunity in the account.

[19]Some military commanders do not know how to adjust
their methods.
They can find an advantageous position.
Still, they cannot use their men effectively.

You must be creative in your planning. 2
You must adapt to your opportunities and weaknesses.
You can use a variety of approaches and still have a consis-
tent result.
You must adjust to a variety of problems and consistently
solve them.

You can deter your potential enemy by using his 3
weaknesses against him.
You can keep your potential enemy's army busy by giving it
work to do.
You can rush your potential enemy by offering him an
advantageous position.

You must make use of war. 4
Do not trust that the enemy isn't coming.
Trust your readiness to meet him.
Do not trust that the enemy won't attack.
Rely only on your ability to pick a place that the enemy can't
attack.

Some salespeople attempt to sell without changing their usual methods.

They can figure out what the key issues are.

Still, they are unable to adjust so they can address them.

2 You must be inventive in planning the sale.

You can find strengths and weaknesses in every situation.

You can use a variety of different approaches and still consistently win sales.

Every situation offers unique problems, but you can always find a good solution.

3 You can overcome competitors by using their weaknesses against them.

You must manipulate your competitors into constantly defending their products.

You can speed the sales process by giving customers a good reason to decide now.

4 You must use your resources carefully.

Do not expect to win any sale without resistance.

Instead, be ready to meet resistance.

Do not trust that competitors won't attack your product.

Instead, structure your sales proposition so that others can't easily attack it.

You can exploit five different faults in a leader. 5
If he is willing to die, you can kill him.
If he wants to survive, you can capture him.
He may have a quick temper.
You can then provoke him with insults.
If he has a delicate sense of honor, you can disgrace him.
If he loves his people, you can create problems for him.
In every situation, look for these five weaknesses.
They are common faults in commanders.
They always lead to military disaster.

[11]To overturn an army, you must kill its general.
To do this, you must use these five weaknesses.
You must always look for them.

✦ ✦ ✦

5 Salespeople can have five different character flaws.
If they are willing to lose a sale, they will lose it.
If they lack courage, they will give products away.
If they have a quick temper, they can be provoked.
If they are sensitive to rejection, they can't ask for an order.
If they are sensitive to criticism, they can be embarrassed.
If they love their arguments, they will get into trouble.
In every situation, look for these five weaknesses.
They are common faults in salespeople.
They can lead to disaster in sales.

These weaknesses can destroy you and your career.
You must know how to exploit them in others.
You must always be aware of them.

Heaven

Moving

Ground

Chapter 9

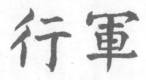

Armed March: Moving Sales Forward

For a salesperson, this chapter serves as a guide to moving the sales process forward despite problems and objections. This long chapter addresses the challenges encountered when moving an organization into new competitive territory. Much of it is dedicated to correctly interpreting signs in the environment.

Sales territories and the rules of dealing with them are different. The chapter's first section covers four different categories of territory and how to navigate them.

You must sell at the right level within an organization. Sun Tzu then briefly addresses the need to control the high ground in whatever type of situation you encounter.

You need to explore the organizations you are selling to. The third section warns about the seasonal and hidden dangers inherent in exploring new territory.

A salesperson must be sensitive to signals. The chapter's fourth section explains various signs in the environment and how to interpret them.

Can you read your competitors' minds? In the long fifth section, Sun Tzu explains in detail how you can determine the conditions and intentions of your opponents by interpreting their behavior.

What do you do when your proposal isn't working? Sun Tzu ends the chapter by describing how to know when you have gone as far as you can go in a new competitive arena and how you can regroup.

Armed March

SUN TZU SAID:

Anyone moving an army must adjust to the enemy. 1
When caught in the mountains, rely on their valleys.
Position yourself on the heights facing the sun.
To win your battles, never attack uphill.
This is how you position your army in the mountains.

6When water blocks you, keep far away from it.
Let the invader cross the river and wait for him.
Do not meet him in midstream.
Wait for him to get half his forces across and then take
advantage of the situation.

10You need to be able to fight.
You can't do that if you are caught in water when you meet
an invader.
Position yourself upstream, facing the sun.
Never face against the current.
Always position your army upstream when near the water.

Moving Sales Forward

1 To move the sale forward, adjust to the customer.
Within large organizations, start low in the organization.
Work up to management and get better known.
To win the sale, never fight upper management.
This is how you work within large hierarchies.

In companies with many divisions, respect their boundaries.
Wait until your competitors cross departmental lines.
Don't copy them in ignoring boundaries.
When they start trying to sell to your contacts, you can easily beat
them.

You must stay competitive.
Don't depend on an organization's internal divisional boundaries
to stop the competition.
Move decisions higher up in the organization.
Make competitors battle the politics of the company.
Always work above them in the organization.

¹⁵You may have to move across marshes.
Move through them quickly without stopping.
You may meet the enemy in the middle of a marsh.
You must keep on the water grasses.
Keep your back to a clump of trees.
This is how you position your army in a marsh.

²¹On a level plateau, take a position that you can change.
Keep the higher ground on your right and to the rear.
Keep danger in front of you and safety behind.
This is how you position yourself on a level plateau.

²⁵You can find an advantage in all four of these situations.
Learn from the great emperor who used positioning to
conquer his four rivals.

Armies are stronger on high ground and weaker on low. 2
They are better camping on sunny southern hillsides than
on shady northern ones.
Provide for your army's health and place men correctly.
Your army will be free from disease.
Done correctly, this means victory.

⁶You must sometimes defend on a hill or riverbank.
You must keep on the south side in the sun.
Keep the uphill slope at your right rear.

⁹This will give the advantage to your army.
It will always give you a position of strength.

Complex organizations can bog you down.
Move quickly through them to find the real decision-maker.
You can encounter competition in confusing organizations.
When you do, try to establish a well-defined sales process.
You don't want the competition to surprise you.
You must avoid missteps in these companies.

In a flat organization, offer flexible proposals.
Move as high as you can to promote your product.
Watch the competition and keep your champions safe.
Champions win sales within flat organizations.

You can win sales in all four types of organizations.
Successful salespeople use the organization to beat their competition.

2 The higher you go within an organization, the stronger you are.
Introduce yourself to the top people as readily as the lower ones.
Healthy relationships come from your value to people.
You must keep your relationships productive.
Do this correctly and you will win customers.

Sometimes you must defend a slight advantage.
Make the value of your product known to the top people.
You always want the top people behind you.

These relationships can only benefit your efforts.
They give you a position of strength.

Stop the march when the rain swells the river into rapids. 3
You may want to ford the river.
Wait until it subsides.

4All regions can have seasonal mountain streams that can
cut you off.
There are seasonal lakes.
There are seasonal blockages.
There are seasonal jungles.
There are seasonal floods.
There are seasonal fissures.
Get away from all these quickly.
Do not get close to them.
Keep them at a distance.
Maneuver the enemy close to them.
Position yourself facing these dangers.
Push the enemy back into them.

16Danger can hide on your army's flank.
There are reservoirs and lakes.
There are reeds and thickets.
There are mountain woods.
Their dense vegetation provides a hiding place.
You must cautiously search through them.
They can always hide an ambush.

3 Stop selling during a change in organizational structure. You can still win the sale.

Wait until company changes resolve themselves.

All organizations have barriers to decision-making that can block your sale.

There are naysayers.

There are gatekeepers.

There are time wasters.

There are deal killers.

There are lawyers.

Get past them quickly.

Do not invest your time in them.

Keep them at a distance.

Put your competition in touch with them.

Keep your eye on these people.

Let your competitors be blindsided by them.

Opposition can be hidden.

Beware of committees.

Beware of task forces.

Beware of bureaucracies.

They can provide a secret base for competitive attack.

You must carefully search through them.

You don't want them to ambush you.

Sometimes, the enemy is close by but remains calm. 4
Expect to find him in a natural stronghold.
Other times he remains at a distance but provokes battle.
He wants you to attack him.

⁵He sometimes shifts the position of his camp.
He is looking for an advantageous position.

⁷The trees in the forest move.
Expect that the enemy is coming.
The tall grasses obstruct your view.
Be suspicious.

¹¹The birds take flight.
Expect that the enemy is hiding.
Animals startle.
Expect an ambush.

¹⁵Notice the dust.
It sometimes rises high in a straight line.
Vehicles are coming.
The dust appears low in a wide band.
Foot soldiers are coming.
The dust seems scattered in different areas.
The enemy is collecting firewood.
Any dust is light and settling down.
The enemy is setting up camp.

4 Competitors are involved in the sale but they are quiet.
You should expect that they have a safe position.
Competitors say little about you but pursue the sale.
They want you to attack their product.

Competitors may make their proposal easy to attack.
Always expect that they have a secret advantage.

The goals of the purchase may suddenly change.
This means that the competition has been active.
There are too many purchasing requirements.
Suspect that the competition is creating them.

Your contacts may suddenly become shy.
Suspect that the competition is planning a surprise.
Your supporters may become uncertain.
The competition is ambushing you.

Listen for rumors about the competition.
News about the competition can come from top managers.
This means that the competition is aggressive.
You hear about your competitors from everywhere.
This means they have many people in the account.
News of competitors is scattered in different areas.
This means that they are learning about the organization.
News of competitors becomes rarer and rarer.
This means that they are inactive.

Your enemy speaks humbly while building up forces. 5
He is planning to advance.

3The enemy talks aggressively and pushes as if to advance.
He is planning to retreat.

5Small vehicles exit his camp first.
They move the army's flanks.
They are forming a battle line.

8Your enemy tries to sue for peace but without offering a
treaty.
He is plotting.

10Your enemy's men run to leave and yet form ranks.
You should expect action.

12Half his army advances and the other half retreats.
He is luring you.

14Your enemy plans to fight but his men just stand there.
They are starving.

16Those who draw water drink it first.
They are thirsty.

18Your enemy sees an advantage but does not advance.
His men are tired.

5 Your competitors seem pessimistic but active.
Expect them to increase pressure.

Your competitors claim victory and attack you.
Expect them to give up soon.

Your competitors ask a prospect for a number of small decisions.
These decisions support their proposal.
Expect them to try to close the sale.

Your competitors offer to give you the sale without anything in return.
Expect them to try to trick you.

Your competitors start actively organizing.
Expect them to call for a decision.

Your competitors offer to split the sale with you.
This means that they are laying a trap.

Your competitors start offering discounts in price.
This means that they aren't making sales.

Your competitors start asking for cash payments.
They are out of money.

Your competitors have a clear opportunity but do nothing.
This means that they are lazy.

²⁰Birds gather.
Your enemy has abandoned his camp.

²²Your enemy's soldiers call in the night.
They are afraid.

²⁴Your enemy's army is raucous.
The men do not take their commander seriously.

²⁶Your enemy's banners and flags shift.
Order is breaking down.

²⁸Your enemy's officers are irritable.
They are exhausted.

³⁰Your enemy's men kill their horses for meat.
They are out of provisions.

³²They don't put their pots away or return to their tents.
They are desperate.

³⁴Enemy troops appear sincere and agreeable.
But their men are slow to speak to each other.
They are no longer united.

³⁷Your enemy offers too many incentives to his men.
He is in trouble.

³⁹Your enemy gives out too many punishments.
His men are weary.

Customers start coming to you.
This means that your competitors have abandoned them.

Competitors ask you for information.
This means that they are afraid.

Competitors' claims are dismissed.
This means that they are not taken seriously.

Competitors' sales proposals suddenly change.
This means that they are disorganized.

Competitors' managers are restless.
This means that their salespeople are ineffective.

Your competitors let their customers dictate terms.
This means that they are out of resources.

Competitors offer desperate proposals.
Expect them to fight you to the end.

Your competitors seem sincere and dedicated.
Nevertheless, their salespeople speak poorly of their management.
This means that they are not dedicated to their company.

Your competitors offer too many incentives to buy.
This means that they are in trouble.

Your competitors start giving customers time limits.
This means that they are under pressure.

[41]Your enemy first acts violently and then is afraid of your larger force.
His best troops have not arrived.

[43]Your enemy comes in a conciliatory manner.
He needs to rest and recuperate.

[45]Your enemy is angry and appears to welcome battle.
This goes on for a long time, but he doesn't attack.
He also doesn't leave the field.
You must watch him carefully.

If you are too weak to fight, you must find more men. 6
In this situation, you must not act aggressively.
You must unite your forces.
Prepare for the enemy.
Recruit men and stay where you are.

[6]You must be cautious about making plans and adjust to the enemy.
You must gather more men.

Your competitors first attack you and then try making friends with you.
This means that they are not too bright.

Competitors try to collaborate with you.
This means that they need your help.

Competitors sell aggressively but do not close the sale.
They are in the sale for a long time, but never attack you.
They never give up the sale either.
In these situations, you must be cautious.

6 If your proposal cannot win the sale, you can build it up.
However, you must not ask the customer for the order.
You must focus your efforts.
You must prepare for the competition.
You must gather information and delay the sale.

You must plan continuously and never take your competitors lightly.
You must never let the competition get ahead of you.

With new, undedicated soldiers, you can depend on 7
them if you discipline them.
They will tend to disobey your orders.
If they do not obey your orders, they will be useless.

4You can depend on seasoned, dedicated soldiers.
But you must avoid disciplining them without reason.
Otherwise, you cannot use them.

7You must control your soldiers with esprit de corps.
You must bring them together by winning victories.
You must get them to believe in you.

10Make it easy for people to know what to do by training
your people.
Your people will then obey you.
If you do not make it easy for people to know what to do,
you won't train your people.
Then they will not obey.

14Make your commands easy to follow.
You must understand the way a crowd thinks.

7 You must offer clear, firm proposals in new customer relationships.
Otherwise, customers will not accept your leadership.
If they do not see your leadership, you have no control.

It is different with established customer relationships.
You must show flexibility.
Your customers serve you best by giving you new ideas.

You must establish strong customer relationships.
You must win customers by making them successful.
They must believe in you.

Make it easy for your customers to buy from you by educating them.
They will then order from you repeatedly.
If you make it difficult for customers to buy, you won't keep your customers.
They will stop listening to you.

You must make it easy to buy.
You must always educate your customers.

Chapter 10

地 形

Field Position: Customer Relationships

As a salesperson, you need a system to help you analyze the types of relationships that you can have with customers. This chapter examines in detail the six characteristics, called field positions that can be used to evaluate your position with a customer, especially in terms of moving to a new position.

What are the important differences in customer positions? Sun Tzu begins the chapter with a detailed description of the six types of field positions and how to utilize them.

What mistakes do salespeople make in dealing with customers? The second section lists the six flaws in organizations and how to diagnose them. Though it is not explained specifically in the text, each of these six flaws arises in and is amplified by the specific field position that corresponds to the order in which it is listed.

How do you know when to move the sale forward or when to close it? In the third section, Sun Tzu examines the issues that you must consider in moving from one temporary position to another.

There is a connection between caring for customers and insisting that they make decisions. In the fourth section, Sun Tzu addresses the proper way of providing leadership to people as you usher them into new situations.

As always, your ability to sell with confidence depends on your knowledge. In the final section, Sun Tzu addresses the need to compare your relative field position with that of your opposite before choosing a course of action.

Field Position

SUN TZU SAID:

Some field positions are unobstructed. 1
Some field positions are entangling.
Some field positions are supporting.
Some field positions are constricted.
Some field positions give you a barricade.
Some field positions are spread out.

7You can attack from some positions easily.
Other forces can meet you easily as well.
We call these unobstructed positions.
These positions are open.
In them, be the first to occupy a high, sunny area.
Put yourself where you can defend your supply routes.
Then you will have an advantage.

Customer Relationships

1 Some customers are accessible.
Some customers are exclusive.
Some customers are supportive.
Some customers are narrow-minded.
Some customers are one-man shows.
Some customers are unqualified.

Notice when customers freely accept you.
They will accept the competition as easily.
These are accessible customers.
These customers are open to new ideas.
With these customers, be the first to understand their needs.
Work with their top people and position products clearly.
With them, leadership is essential.

¹⁴You can attack from some positions easily.
Disaster arises when you try to return to them.
These are entangling positions.
These field positions are one-sided.
Wait until your enemy is unprepared.
You can then attack from these positions and win.
Avoid a well-prepared enemy.
You will try to attack and lose.
Since you can't return, you will meet disaster.
These field positions offer no advantage.

²⁴You cannot leave some positions without losing an
advantage.
If the enemy leaves this ground, he also loses an advantage.
We call these supporting field positions.
These positions strengthen you.
The enemy may try to entice you away.
Still, hold your position.
You must entice the enemy to leave.
You then strike him as he is leaving.
These field positions offer an advantage.

³³Some field positions are constricted.
Get to these positions first.
You must fill these areas and await the enemy.
Sometimes, the enemy will reach them first.
If he fills them, do not follow him.
However, if he fails to fill them, you can go after him.

Some customers give you one shot at getting their business.

You cannot go back to them after striking out.

These are exclusive customers.

They give you one chance.

Wait and identify an issue that requires your help.

You can then go after them and win their business.

Avoid selling to them if you don't solve a real problem.

Your attempts will fail.

Since you can't come back, you will waste your only chance.

You cannot control these customers.

Some customers judge proposals by which salesperson is the most confident.

Neither you nor your competition can retreat without losing.

These are supportive customers.

These customers make you a better salesperson.

You may get discouraged dealing with them.

You must stick with your proposal.

Encourage competitors to lose patience.

Then criticize them when they relent.

You want this type of customer.

Some customers are narrow-minded.

You must contact these customers first.

You must influence them and then wait for the competition.

Competitors may contact them first.

If they win over the decision-makers, don't waste your time.

But if they fail to win them, you can go after them.

39Some field positions give you a barricade.
Get to these positions first.
You must occupy their southern, sunny heights in order to
await the enemy.
Sometimes the enemy occupies these areas first.
If so, entice him away.
Never go after him.

45Some field positions are too spread out.
Your force may seem equal to the enemy.
Still you will lose if you provoke a battle.
If you fight, you will not have any advantage.

49These are the six types of field positions.
Each battleground has its own rules.
As a commander, you must know where to go.
You must examine each position closely.

Some armies can be outmaneuvered. 2
Some armies are too lax.
Some armies fall down.
Some armies fall apart.
Some armies are disorganized.
Some armies must retreat.

7Know all six of these weaknesses.
They create weak timing and disastrous positions.
They all arise from the army's commander.

Some customers are one-man shows.
You must contact the decision-maker first.
After you contact the main decision-maker, you can then invite in the competition.
Sometimes competitors get to the head person first.
If so, lure the decision-maker away from them.
Do not try to sell to them if competitors have won the top person.

Some customers are unqualified.
It may seem like you can convince them to buy.
But you are wasting your time selling to them.
Even if you make a sale, you will never benefit from it.

These are the six types of customers.
Each customer type has its own rules.
You must know who your customers are.
You must never stop asking questions.

2 There are salespeople who rush.
There are salespeople who are too slow.
There are salespeople who stumble.
There are salespeople who fall apart.
There are salespeople who are disorganized.
There are salespeople who give up.

You must avoid these six weaknesses.
These problems don't arise from your nature.
They come from your actions.

¹⁰One general can command a force equal to the enemy.
Still his enemy outflanks him.
This means that his army can be outmaneuvered.

¹³Another can have strong soldiers but weak officers.
This means that his army is too lax.

¹⁵Another has strong officers but weak soldiers.
This means that his army will fall down.

¹⁷Another has subcommanders that are angry and defiant.
They attack the enemy and fight their own battles.
The commander cannot know the battlefield.
This means that his army will fall apart.

²¹Another general is weak and easygoing.
He fails to make his orders clear.
His officers and men lack direction.
This shows in his military formations.
This means that his army is disorganized.

²⁶Another general fails to predict the enemy.
He pits his small forces against larger ones.
His weak forces attack stronger ones.
He fails to pick his fights correctly.
This means that his army must retreat.

Your products may equal those of the competition.
Still, you let the competition outmaneuver you.
This means that you are in a rush.

Your ideas are good but your process is weak.
You will be too slow.

Your process is strong but your ideas are weak.
You will stumble.

You can neglect your sales contacts.
The people in the account don't help you.
Then you fail to get to know the customer.
You will fall apart.

You can be lazy and sloppy.
Your proposal is unclear.
If your proposal is unclear, customers lack direction.
Your time is not well spent.
You are disorganized.

As a salesperson, you can fail to understand your customers.
You offer solutions to problems they don't have.
You compete on the wrong issues.
You fail to pick the right customers.
You must eventually give up.

³¹You must know all about these six weaknesses.
You must understand the philosophies that lead to defeat.
When a general arrives, you can know what he will do.
You must study each general carefully.

You must control your field position. 3
It will always strengthen your army.

³You must predict the enemy to overpower him and win.
You must analyze the obstacles, dangers, and distances.
This is the best way to command.

⁶Understand your field position before you meet opponents.
Then you will succeed.
You can fail to understand your field position and meet
opponents.
Then you will fail.

¹⁰You must provoke battle when you will certainly win.
It doesn't matter what you are ordered.
The government may order you not to fight.
Despite that, you must always fight when you will win.

¹⁴Sometimes provoking a battle will lead to a loss.
The government may order you to fight.
Despite that, you must avoid battle when you will lose.

You must understand all six faults.
In order to win sales, you must avoid these weaknesses.
You must understand your customers.
The customer helps you make the sale.

3 You must guide the customer.
This always strengthens your position.

You must foresee how to discredit the buyer's alternatives.
You must see the buyer's difficulties, problems, and needs.
This is the best way to win sales.

Understand your buyer's needs when you try to close the sale.
If you do, you will always win the sale.
You may not understand your buyer's interests and try to close the sale.
But you will fail.

You must close when you are certain to get the sale.
Don't try to time the sale to meet your company's needs.
There may be many reasons why the timing isn't ideal.
Still, you must always close when the opportunity is there.

When you will lose the sale, you must delay the decision.
Your boss may insist that you try to close the sale.
Still, you must prevent the decision when you will lose.

[17]You must advance without desiring praise.
You must retreat without fearing shame.
The only correct move is to preserve your troops.
This is how you serve your country.
This is how you reward your nation.

Think of your soldiers as little children. 4
You can make them follow you into a deep river.
Treat them as your beloved children.
You can lead them all to their deaths.

[5]Some leaders are generous but cannot use their men.
They love their men but cannot command them.
Their men are unruly and disorganized.
These leaders create spoiled children.
Their soldiers are useless.

You may know what your soldiers will do in an attack. 5
You may not know if the enemy is vulnerable to attack.
You will then win only half the time.
You may know that the enemy is vulnerable to attack.
You may not know if your men have the capability of
attacking him.
You will still win only half the time.
You may know that the enemy is vulnerable to attack.
You may know that your men are ready to attack.
You may not, however, know how to position yourself in the
field for battle.
You will still win only half the time.

You must never close because you need the commission.
You must close without worrying that you will be rejected.
You should worry only about preserving your advantages.
You must help the customer in order to serve your own company.
This is how you make yourself successful.

4 Treat your customers as your children.
They will follow you.
Treat them with care and attention.
They will stay with you forever.

If you care about your customers, you must ask them to buy.
If you love them, you must demand that they act.
You must not leave them confused—without guidance.
You cannot help them if they don't listen.
Your support is useless.

5 You can know that you have good products.
But you must also know their value to customers.
If you don't, you have done only part of your job.
You can know how to satisfy customers' needs.
But you must still convince customers that your proposal is the best.
If you don't, you have done only part of your job.
You can know customers' needs.
You can know how your products serve their needs.
But you must also know exactly what your customers are thinking about their choices.
If you don't, you have done only part of your job.

[11]You must know how to make war.
You can then act without confusion.
You can attempt anything.

[14]We say:
Know the enemy and know yourself.
Your victory will be painless.
Know the weather and the field.
Your victory will be complete.

✦ ✦ ✦

You must truly understand selling.
You can then act with certainty.
You can sell anything.

Pay attention:
Know your customers and your products.
Then sales are effortless.
Understand customers' thinking and their needs.
Then your success is assured.

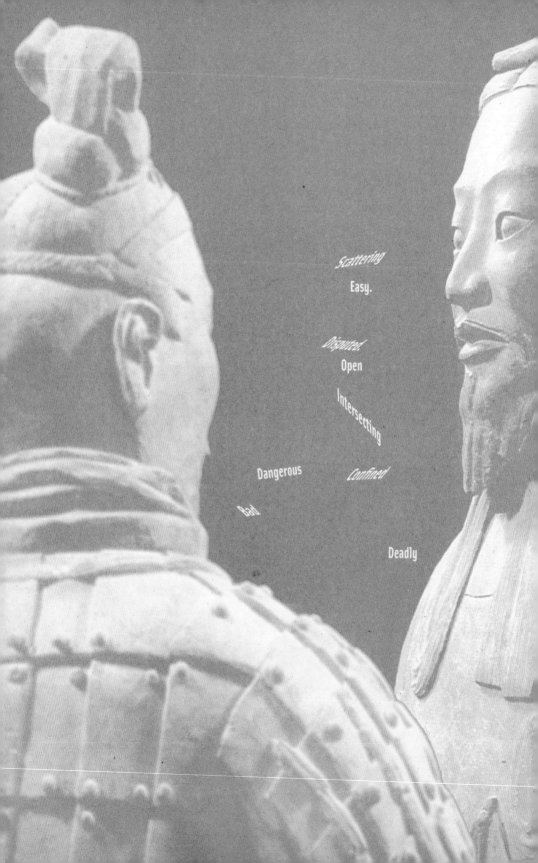

Scattering

Easy.

Disputed

Open

Intersecting

Dangerous

Confined

Bad

Deadly

Chapter 11

九地

Types of Terrain: Sales Situations

For a salesperson, this chapter's nine stages describe the nine different phases through which a sales process commonly evolves. Campaigns tend to evolve as an army penetrates ever more deeply into enemy territory. The types of terrain described here chart that evolotion. Each of these stages of development requires a clear tactical response.

What stage is your sales campaign currently in? The chapter's first section describes the nine campaign stages and the specific tactical focuses that they demand.

For early stages, Sun Tzu describes how to keep opponents from organizing and how to defend against invasion.

Things change when you go after new accounts. The third section discusses the general management of an invasion into enemy territory.

Sun Tzu then addresses how to prepare the right response to attack beforehand and how to use adversity to unite your forces.

He then discusses the functions of a leader.

In the sixth section, Sun Tzu reviews the stages of a campaign, with an emphasis on troop psychology.

Sun Tzu then emphasizes knowledge and unity as the keys to a successful campaign, with a special emphasis on the ability to recover from initial setbacks.

The final section addresses the need to set the proper tone for a campaign at the very start.

Types of Terrain

SUN TZU SAID:

Use the art of war. 1
Know when the terrain will scatter you.
Know when the terrain is easy.
Know when the terrain is disputed.
Know when the terrain is open.
Know when the terrain is intersecting.
Know when the terrain is dangerous.
Know when the terrain is bad.
Know when the terrain is confined.
Know when the terrain is deadly.

[11]Warring parties must sometimes fight inside their own
territory.
This is scattering terrain.

[13]When you enter hostile territory, your penetration is shallow.
This is easy terrain.

[15]Some terrain gives you an advantageous position.
But it gives others an advantageous position as well.
This will be disputed terrain.

Sales Situations

1 Use your sales skills:
Know when your sales situation is tenuous.
Know when your sales situation is easy.
Know when your sales situation is contentious.
Know when your sales situation is open.
Know when your sales situation is shared.
Know when your sales situation is serious.
Know when your sales situation is bad.
Know when your sales situation is restricting.
Know when your sales situation is desperate.

All customers are initially uneasy and distrustful with a new salesperson.
This is a tenuous situation.

The customer is open to a sales call.
This is an easy situation.

The customer shows some interest.
However, he or she shows interest in competing products as well.
This is a contentious situation.

[18]You can use some terrain to advance easily.
Others can advance along with you.
This is open terrain.

[21]Everyone shares access to a given area.
The first one to arrive there can gather a larger group than
anyone else.
This is intersecting terrain.

[24]You can penetrate deeply into hostile territory.
Then many hostile cities are behind you.
This is dangerous terrain.

[27]There are mountain forests.
There are dangerous obstructions.
There are reservoirs.
Everyone confronts these obstacles on a campaign.
They make bad terrain.

[32]In some areas, the entry passage is narrow.
You are closed in as you try to get out of them.
In this type of area, a few people can effectively attack your
much larger force.
This is confined terrain.

[36]You can sometimes survive only if you fight quickly.
You will die if you delay.
This is deadly terrain.

You make easy progress in the sale.

The competition, however, can still come in at any time.

This is an open situation.

Complementary companies can work together on a sale.

The first one in the account can determine the priorities in the sales process.

This is a shared situation.

You invest a great deal of time in a sale.

The closer you get to closing, the more the customer resists.

This is a serious situation.

Some customers can't pay.

Others can't decide.

You can't make some customers happy.

These are serious problems in any sale.

These are bad situations.

Getting into many sales is difficult.

Getting out of some sales, however, is impossible.

You must make commitments that limit what you can and cannot do.

These are restricting situations.

Sometimes you can win a sale only if you close immediately.

You will lose the sale if the process continues.

These are do-or-die situations.

³⁹To be successful, you must control scattering terrain by
avoiding battle.
Control easy terrain by not stopping.
Control disputed terrain by not attacking.
Control open terrain by staying with the enemy's forces.
Control intersecting terrain by uniting with your allies.
Control dangerous terrain by plundering.
Control bad terrain by keeping on the move.
Control confined terrain by using surprise.
Control deadly terrain by fighting.

Go to an area that is known to be good for waging war. 2
Use it to cut off the enemy's contact between his front and
back lines.
Prevent his small parties from relying on his larger force.
Stop his strong divisions from rescuing his weak ones.
Prevent his officers from getting their men together.
Chase his soldiers apart to stop them from amassing.
Harass them to prevent their ranks from forming.

⁸When joining battle gives you an advantage, you must do it.
When it isn't to your benefit, you must avoid it.

¹⁰A daring soldier may ask:
"A large, organized enemy army and its general are coming.
What do I do to prepare for them?"

To be successful in tenuous situations, avoid creating even a little resistance.

In easy situations, don't stop.

In contentious situations, don't press for a decision.

In open situations, don't try to block the competition.

In shared situations, bring in your handpicked allies.

In serious situations, move confidently and as fast as possible.

In bad situations, get out and find another customer.

In restricting situations, look for alternatives.

In do-or-die situations, demand the order.

2 Find any area where you can help the customer.

You must control the flow of information to the customer about the market.

Keep the competition from developing many supporters.

Keep different competitors at odds with one another.

Prevent them from getting together against you.

Discredit their proposals before they can gain credibility.

Discredit the company if the proposal seems acceptable.

When you have the advantage, force a confrontation.

When you don't have the advantage, avoid confrontation.

You may ask:

"A large, well-organized competitor is coming into my sale. What should I do?"

¹³Tell him:

"First seize an area that the enemy must have.

Then he will pay attention to you.

Mastering speed is the essence of war.

Take advantage of a large enemy's inability to keep up.

Use a philosophy of avoiding difficult situations.

Attack the area where he doesn't expect you."

You must use the philosophy of an invader. 3

Invade deeply and then concentrate your forces.

This controls your men without oppressing them.

⁴Get your supplies from the riches of the territory.

They are sufficient to supply your whole army.

⁶Take care of your men and do not overtax them.

Your esprit de corps increases your momentum.

Keep your army moving and plan for surprises.

Make it difficult for the enemy to count your forces.

Position your men where there is no place to run.

They will then face death without fleeing.

They will find a way to survive.

Your officers and men will fight to their utmost.

¹⁴Military officers who are committed lose their fear.

When they have nowhere to run, they must stand firm.

Deep in enemy territory, they are captives.

Since they cannot escape, they will fight.

Pay attention.

Raise issues that customers must address quickly.

You can then guide them.

Urgency is the essence of sales.

Take advantage of a large competitor's inability to keep up.

Act without hesitation.

Keep the discussion where the competition is unprepared.

3 Act like a guest when you go into the customer's business.
When you invest your time, you must focus your efforts.

You must help the customer's people; do not fight them.

You must get your support from internal champions.

The customer's needs must fuel your sales efforts.

Build support for your product, but do not oversell it.

Make customers feel like a vital part of your company.

Keep the sales process moving and expect surprises.

Always give customers more value than they expect.

Put yourself in a position in which you must make the sale.

You cannot just go on to the next prospect.

You must find a way to help the prospect you have.

You must commit all of your skills to win.

When you commit yourself, you lose your fear of rejection.

When you must win, you can be firm with customers.

When you are dedicated to customers, you have no choice.

You have no choice but to do everything you can.

[18]Commit your men completely.
Without being posted, they will be on guard.
Without being asked, they will get what is needed.
Without being forced, they will be dedicated.
Without being given orders, they can be trusted.

[23]Stop them from guessing by removing all their doubts.
Stop them from dying by giving them no place to run.

[25]Your officers may not be rich.
Nevertheless, they still desire plunder.
They may die young.
Nevertheless, they still want to live forever.

[29]You must order the time of attack.
Officers and men may sit and weep until their lapels are wet.
When they stand up, tears may stream down their cheeks.
Put them in a position where they cannot run.
They will show the greatest courage under fire.

Make good use of war. 4
This demands instant reflexes.
You must develop these instant reflexes.
Act like an ordinary mountain snake.
If people strike your head then stop them with your tail.
If they strike your tail then stop them with your head.
If they strike your middle then use both your head and tail.

Totally commit yourself.

Without being warned, you must be on guard.

Without being asked, you must answer expected questions.

Without being forced, you must consider customer needs.

Without being told, you must take initiative.

Stop second-guessing yourself and stay well informed.

Give yourself no excuse for losing and you will stop losing sales.

Your efforts may fail.

This isn't because you can't make them successful.

You have failed before.

It wasn't because you didn't want to win customer business.

You must decide when to close the sale.

You may feel shy and uncertain.

When you must ask for the order, you may fear rejection.

Put yourself in a position where you must win the sale.

You will find the courage you need.

4 Make good use of your selling.

You must respond with practiced precision.

You must prepare to instantly overcome objections.

You should be able to act on reflex.

Some will challenge your product's quality; attack with its value.

Others will challenge your product's value; attack with its quality.

They can challenge on mediocrity; attack with its value and quality.

[8]A daring soldier asks:
"Can any army imitate these instant reflexes?"
We answer:
"It can."

[12]To command and get the most out of proud people, you
must study adversity.
People work together when they are in the same boat during
a storm.
In this situation, one rescues the other just as the right
hand helps the left.

[15]Use adversity correctly.
Tether your horses and bury your wagon's wheels.
Still, you can't depend on this alone.
An organized force is braver than lone individuals.
This is the art of organization.
Put the tough and weak together.
You must also use the terrain.

[22]Make good use of war.
Unite your men as one.
Never let them give up.

The commander must be a military professional. 5
This requires confidence and detachment.
You must maintain dignity and order.
You must control what your men see and hear.
They must follow you without knowing your plans.

You may question this.
Can you sell using such instant responses?
There is only one answer.
You must!

To lead customers when they want to be in charge, you must study their problems.
They will work with you if both of you realize that you need each other.
You can help each other if you realize that you are partners in business.

You must lead customers correctly.
You want them to feel the need for your product.
This isn't, however, enough.
Give them a balanced picture so you win their confidence.
This is the art of persuasion.
You must show both your strengths and weaknesses.
You must know what is important.

Use your time well.
Make your presentation simple and focused.
You must never give up.

5 You must dedicate yourself to being a salesperson.
This requires confidence and detachment.
You must maintain your authority and control.
You must inspire your customers' vision and ideas.
They must believe you know more than they do.

⁶You can reinvent your men's roles.

You can change your plans.

You can use your men without their understanding.

⁹You must shift your campgrounds.

You must take detours from the ordinary routes.

You must use your men without giving them your strategy.

¹²A commander provides what is needed now.

This is like climbing high and being willing to kick away your ladder.

You must be able to lead your men deep into different surrounding territory.

And yet, you can discover the opportunity to win.

¹⁶You must drive men like a flock of sheep.

You must drive them to march.

You must drive them to attack.

You must never let them know where you are headed.

You must unite them into a great army.

You must then drive them against all opposition.

This is the job of a true commander.

²³You must adapt to the different terrain.

You must adapt to find an advantage.

You must manage your people's affections.

You must study all these skills.

You must find new possibilities in customers' businesses.

You must invent new approaches.

You must try new ideas without the assurance of success.

You must offer a different proposal for every customer.

You must offer something different from your competition.

The customer should never anticipate you.

You must provide exactly what is needed at the moment.

You must be willing to go out on a limb and take a risk when selling.

You must become deeply involved in your customers' business to discover their problems.

These problems create the opportunities that will win the sale.

You must inspire customers to act.

You must inspire them to throw away the old.

You must inspire them to try something new.

You must never let them know where you are headed.

You must focus your proposals on critical issues.

You must overcome all objections.

This is the job of a true salesperson.

You must adapt to every sales situation.

You must adjust your methods to win the sale.

You must control customers' emotions.

You must master all these skills.

Always use the philosophy of invasion. 6
Deep invasions concentrate your forces.
Shallow invasions scatter your forces.
When you leave your country and cross the border, you must
take control.
This is always critical ground.
You can sometimes move in any direction.
This is always intersecting ground.
You can penetrate deeply into a territory.
This is always dangerous ground.
You penetrate only a little way.
This is always easy ground.
Your retreat is closed and the path ahead tight.
This is always confined ground.
There is sometimes no place to run.
This is always deadly ground.

[16]To use scattering terrain correctly, you must inspire your
men's devotion.
On easy terrain, you must keep in close communication.
On disputed terrain, you try to hamper the enemy's progress.
On open terrain, you must carefully defend your chosen position.
On intersecting terrain, you must solidify your alliances.
On dangerous terrain, you must ensure your food supplies.
On bad terrain, you must keep advancing along the road.
On confined terrain, you must stop information leaks from
your headquarters.
On deadly terrain, you must show what you can do by
killing the enemy.

6 You must act like a guest in a prospect's business.
In long sales cycles, focus your efforts on a few key ideas.
In short sales cycles, work with many prospects at once.
When you commit yourself to a customer, you must offer leadership.
This is a critical moment.
You can go to different departments.
Look for allies who share your goals.
You eventually reach the end of the process.
Expect serious objections.
You won't see objections at the beginning of the sale.
This is always the easy part of the sale.
Then your choices become fewer and more difficult.
These are restricting situations.
You must eventually close the sale.
This is a do-or-die situation.

To succeed in tenuous situations, you must get customers excited.
In easy situations, you must meet often with customers.
In contentious situations, you must create obstacles for your competitors.
In open situations, you must defend your specific proposal.
In shared situations, you must control your partners.
In serious situations, you must have plenty of resources.
In bad situations, you must go on to another customer.
In restricting situations, you must defend your bottom line with the top decision-makers.
In do-or-die situations, you must prove yourself by winning the order.

²⁵Make your men feel like an army.
Surround them and they will defend themselves.
If they cannot avoid it, they will fight.
If they are under pressure, they will obey.

Do the right thing when you don't know your 7
different enemies' plans.
Don't attempt to meet them.

³You don't know the position of mountain forests, dangerous
obstructions, and reservoirs?
Then you cannot march the army.
You don't have local guides?
You won't get any of the benefits of the terrain.

⁷There are many factors in war.
You may lack knowledge of any one of them.
If so, it is wrong to take a nation into war.

¹⁰You must be able to control your government's war.
If you divide a big nation, it will be unable to put together a
large force.
Increase your enemy's fear of your ability.
Prevent his forces from getting together and organizing.

Shape your presentations to the customers' beliefs.
If you pressure them, they will fight you.
When you make it easy, they will buy.
When they need you, they will follow your lead.

7 Do the right thing when you don't understand your prospects' businesses.
Admit that you aren't prepared to sell to them.

You don't really understand a certain prospect's organization and its needs?
Then you can't move that sale forward.
You don't have information from within the company?
You won't know anyone's goals or needs.

There is so much to know.
You don't want to miss anything.
Otherwise, you won't control the results in the sale.

You must control everything in the sale.
Attack real problems before customers develop their own solutions to them.
Get customers worried about their business.
Answer their questions so that they can't form objections.

¹⁴Do the right thing and do not arrange outside alliances
before their time.
You will not have to assert your authority prematurely.
Trust only yourself and your self-interest.
This increases the enemy's fear of you.
You can make one of his allies withdraw.
His whole nation can fall.

²⁰Distribute rewards without worrying about having a system.
Halt without the government's command.
Attack with the whole strength of your army.
Use your army as if it were a single man.

²⁴Attack with skill.
Do not discuss it.
Attack when you have an advantage.
Do not talk about the dangers.
When you can launch your army into deadly ground, even if
it stumbles, it can still survive.
You can be weakened in a deadly battle and yet be stronger
afterward.

³⁰Even a large force can fall into misfortune.
If you fall behind, however, you can still turn defeat into victory.
You must use the skills of war.
To survive, you must adapt yourself to your enemy's purpose.
You must stay with him no matter where he goes.
It may take a thousand miles to kill the general.
If you correctly understand him, you can find the skill to do it.

Do the right thing and don't look for business allies to help with every sale.

You won't have to fight for control.

Trust only yourself and your own resources.

This increases your customers' dependence on you.

You can convince competitors' allies to abandon them.

Their whole sales effort may then fail.

Working alone, you don't divide the profits.

You can change your proposal without negotiating.

You can focus all your resources.

You can work toward a single goal.

You win sales for business reasons.

Don't brag about your wins.

You are judged by the number of sales you win.

Don't worry about the ones you lose.

You can get into bad situations and lose sales, but you can still survive.

You may temporarily lose ground, but you can also learn from your mistakes.

You can win many times and still get into bad situations.

If you fall behind, however, you can still turn defeat into success.

You need to develop a professional attitude.

To sell, you must adapt completely to customers' needs.

You must stay with customers no matter where they go.

You can invest months of time to win them.

If you are skillful, you can completely understand their businesses.

Manage your government correctly at the start of a war. 8
Close your borders and tear up passports.
Block the passage of envoys.
Encourage the halls of power to rise to the occasion.
You must use any means to put an end to politics.
Your enemy's people will leave you an opening.
You must instantly invade through it.

8Immediately seize a place that they love.
Do it quickly.
Trample any border to pursue the enemy.
Use your judgment about when to fight.

12Doing the right thing at the start of war is like
approaching a woman.
Your enemy's men must open the door.
After that, you should act like a streaking rabbit.
The enemy will be unable to catch you.

◆ ◆ ◆

8 Do the right things at the beginning of a sale.
Keep quiet and forget past proposals.
Don't try to negotiate.
Encourage the top decision-makers to rise to the occasion.
These are the people you must influence.
The customer will eventually give you an opportunity.
You must seize it quickly.

Quickly focus on goals that customers want to achieve.
Waste no time.
Don't be afraid of barriers while pursuing the sale.
Use your judgment about when to sell.

You should begin every sales situation by carefully playing hard to get.
The customer will eventually give you an opening.
After that, you should act quickly and unpredictably.
The competition will be unable to catch up with you.

♦ ♦ ♦

Chapter 12

Attacking with Fire: Using Desire

For the salesperson, the lessons in this chapter offer a complete plan for leveraging factors in the environment to increase prospects' desire for your product. Although Sun Tzu uses this chapter to discuss a specific weapon, fire, its broader subject is using any weapon, with an emphasis on leveraging forces in the environment as weapons. Our sales interpretation is based on the fact that people desire what they see in their larger environment.

What types of desires should you think about in making a sale? Sun Tzu begins by describing the five specific targets for environmental attack. He also addresses the critical importance of timing in these attacks.

How you leverage a customer's desires depends on his or her reactions to what you say. The second section in this chapter emphasizes that the attack itself is less important than the response to it. An attack does not create an opportunity. It is the response to it that creates the opportunity.

The logic of persuasion is less important than the emotion of desire. Both are needed in selling. In the third section, Sun Tzu briefly compares using fire and water as environmental weapons.

Sales is the most emotionally demanding job in business. Sun Tzu ends his discussion of fire and desire with the need to control emotional responses in both undertaking and responding to attacks.

Attacking with Fire

There are five ways of attacking with fire. 1
The first is burning troops.
The second is burning supplies.
The third is burning supply transport.
The fourth is burning storehouses.
The fifth is burning camps.

7To make fire, you must have the resources.
To build a fire, you must prepare the raw materials.

9To attack with fire, you must be in the right season.
To start a fire, you must have the time.

11Choose the right season.
The weather must be dry.

13Choose the right time.
Pick a season when the grass is as high as the side of a cart.

15You can tell the proper days by the stars in the night sky.
You want days when the wind rises in the morning.

Using Desire

1 There are five categories of customer desires:
The first is personal needs.
The second is the need for products.
The third is the need for information.
The fourth is the need for profit.
The fifth is the need for people.

To create desire, a product must have value to a customer.
To stimulate desire, you must know the customer's mind.

To sell using that desire, you must make customers feel their needs.
To close using desire, you must pick the right moment.

There is a right time to close the sale.
It is when customers' needs are at their peak.

Choose the right time to close sales.
Pick a time when customers have plenty of money.

To know the right time, read the customers' signals.
You want to pick a time that gives you influence.

Everyone attacks with fire. 2

You must create five different situations with fire and be able
to adjust to them.

3You start a fire inside the enemy's camp.
Then attack the enemy's periphery.

5You launch a fire attack, but the enemy remains calm.
Wait and do not attack.

7The fire reaches its height.
Follow its path if you can.
If you can't follow it, stay where you are.

10Spreading fires on the outside of camp can kill.
You can't always get fire inside the enemy's camp.
Take your time in spreading it.

13Set the fire when the wind is at your back.
Don't attack into the wind.
Daytime winds last a long time.
Night winds fade quickly.

17Every army must know how to adjust to the five possible
attacks by fire.
Use many men to guard against them.

2 Everyone tries to address customer needs.
You can stimulate five different types of customer needs and adjust
to them.

You may address a central need of the company.
Then you can deal with peripheral issues.

You uncover a need that doesn't worry customers.
Wait until they become concerned before you sell.

Some customers' needs demand attention now.
Present solutions immediately if you can.
If you can't address these issues, wait for a better time.

Publicizing needs can win sales.
In many situations, you can't get to the decision-maker.
Take your time promoting your solution.

You can fan customer desires.
Don't fight against prevailing attitudes.
Well-known needs get attention.
Subtle needs are easily overlooked.

You must master these five methods of harnessing customer
desires.
Your sales process must prepare you to use them.

When you use fire to assist your attacks, you are clever. 3
Water can add force to an attack.
You can also use water to disrupt an enemy's forces.
It does not, however, take his resources.

You win in battle by getting the opportunity to attack. 4
It is dangerous if you fail to study how to accomplish this
achievement.
As commander, you cannot waste your opportunities.

4We say:
A wise leader plans success.
A good general studies it.
If there is little to be gained, don't act.
If there is little to win, do not use your men.
If there is no danger, don't fight.

10As the leader, you cannot let your anger interfere with the
success of your forces.
As commander, you cannot let yourself become enraged
before you go to battle.
Join the battle only when it is in your advantage to act.
If there is no advantage in joining a battle, stay put.

14Anger can change back into happiness.
Rage can change back into joy.
A nation once destroyed cannot be brought back to life.
Dead men do not return to the living.

3 Leveraging customer desires to generate sales is smart selling.
Persuasion can help you sell.

You can use persuasion to involve customers.

Persuasion alone, however, doesn't create dependence.

4 You win customers by selling your strengths.
Additionally, you must carefully nurture your relationships with them.

In sales, you cannot afford to waste your efforts.

Pay attention!

If you are clever, you plan to win customers.

If you are truly clever, you plan to keep them.

If customers have no long-term value, don't sell to them.

If customers can't buy, don't waste your time.

If customers have no problems, don't sell to them.

You must never let your need for money affect how you deal with a prospect.

As a salesperson, you must never try to close a sale because your ego desires a success.

Sell only when it is to your long-term advantage to sell.

If there is no benefit in selling, find another prospect.

Greed can change to poverty.

Pride can be easily humbled.

If you waste your time, you will not get it back.

Worthless customers cannot make you successful.

[18]This fact must make a wise leader cautious.
A good general is on guard.

[20]Your philosophy must be to keep the nation peaceful and
the army intact.

✦ ✦ ✦

Knowing this, you must be selective.
You must always watch for the best opportunities.

Your plan must be to pick the right customers and build your territory.

♦ ♦ ♦

Knowing

Chapter 13

用 間

Using Spies: Using Questions

As a salesperson, you need to know how to use questions to gather information. In his final chapter, Sun Tzu addresses what he considers to be the most important element of strategy: information. A number of earlier chapters address the importance of information in their closing sections; here, in the closing chapter, Sun Tzu returns to that topic with a special emphasis on developing sources of information.

Not asking the right questions in the sales process is extremely expensive. Sun Tzu begins by describing the many costs of war that can be minimized by the right information. He makes the point that this information must come from people as sources.

How many basic kinds of questions do you need to ask? Sun Tzu uses the second section to list the five different types of information and their sources.

There are rules for using questions in sales. The third section of this chapter discusses techniques for evaluating information and managing information sources.

In sales, it is often the details that matter. This chapter's fourth section teaches that before you tackle a specific problem you must first find sources that provide a complete picture of that problem.

The past is the key to your sales future. The closing section points out that the history of competition shows that success depends first on the cultivation of good information sources. For salespeople, this means knowing how to ask good questions.

Using Spies

SUN TZU SAID:

All successful armies require thousands of men. 1
They invade and march thousands of miles.
Whole families are destroyed.
Other families must be heavily taxed.
Every day, a large amount of money must be spent.

6Internal and external events force people to move.
They are unable to work while on the road.
They are unable to find and hold a useful job.
This affects 70 percent of thousands of families.

10You can watch and guard for years.
Then a single battle can determine victory in a day.
Despite this, bureaucrats worship the value of their salary
money too dearly.
They remain ignorant of the enemy's condition.
The result is cruel.

15They are not leaders of men.
They are not servants of the state.
They are not masters of victory.

Using Questions

1 Becoming a successful salesperson requires effort.
You have to travel thousands of miles.
You waste months of time.
Someone must pay for your efforts.
Every day, it costs money.

When you are selling, customer contact moves the process forward.
You waste your time if you are not talking to customers.
You can't always make progress in a sale.
Still, tremendous resources are required to support you.

You can work on a sale for years.
Then it can be decided in a single day.
Despite this, too many salespeople are too selfish with investing their time.
You cannot afford to stay ignorant about the customer.
Thinking you don't have the time to learn is foolishness.

Without information, you cannot guide the sale.
You are of no help to your company.
You cannot win sales.

[18]You need a creative leader and a worthy commander.
You must move your troops to the right places to beat others.
You must accomplish your attack and escape unharmed.
This requires foreknowledge.
You can obtain foreknowledge.
You can't get it from demons or spirits.
You can't see it from professional experience.
You can't check it with analysis.
You can only get it from other people.
You must always know the enemy's situation.

You must use five types of spies. 2
You need local spies.
You need inside spies.
You need double agents.
You need doomed spies.
You need surviving spies.

[7]You need all five types of spies.
No one must discover your methods.
You will then be able to put together a true picture.
This is the commander's most valuable resource.

[11]You need local spies.
Get them by hiring people from the countryside.

[13]You need inside spies.
Win them by subverting government officials.

You must be an intelligent, valuable leader.

You must spend time on the right issues to win any sale.

You must win your sales in a minimum of time.

This requires information.

You can get this information.

You won't get it from psychology.

You won't get it from past experience.

You can't reason it out.

You can only get it by asking questions of people.

You must always learn the customer's issues.

2 There are only five types of questions.

There are qualifying questions.

There are identifying questions.

There are value questions.

There are leading questions.

There are closing questions.

You must use all five types of questions.

If you do, no one will ever challenge your knowledge.

You can learn about any business and its workings.

This information is your most valuable resource.

You must ask qualifying questions.

Ask everyone about the basic condition of the business.

You must ask identifying questions.

Discover who makes the decisions within the organization.

¹⁵You need double agents.
Discover enemy agents and convert them.

¹⁷You need doomed spies.
Deceive professionals into being captured.
Let them know your orders.
They then take those orders to your enemy.

²¹You need surviving spies.
Someone must return with a report.

Your job is to build a complete army. 3
No relations are as intimate as the ones with spies.
No rewards are too generous for spies.
No work is as secret as that of spies.

⁵If you aren't clever and wise, you can't use spies.
If you aren't fair and just, you can't use spies.
If you can't see the small subtleties, you won't get the truth
from spies.

⁸Pay attention to small, trifling details!
Spies are helpful in every area.

¹⁰Spies are the first to hear information, so they must not
spread information.
Spies who give your location or talk to others must be killed
along with those to whom they have talked.

You must ask value questions.
Discover what is important to customers and focus on it.

You must ask leading questions.
Ask questions that guide customers in a certain direction.
You don't tell them what you want them to believe.
You ask questions that lead them to think it themselves.

You must ask closing questions.
These are the questions that create the sale.

3 Your job is to create a good sale.
You can create close customer relationships with questions.
No other skill is as valuable.
No other words should be as carefully prepared.

Questions do not work without the use of common sense.
You must ask only fair and reasonable questions.
You must listen carefully to discover the real value of asking questions.

You must pay very careful attention.
You can learn everything from asking the right question.

Questions are the fastest way to get information, but you must listen.
Salespeople who talk before they have thoroughly listened hurt themselves and their customers.

You may want to attack an army's position. 4
You may want to attack a certain fortification.
You may want to kill people in a certain place.
You must first know the guarding general.
You must know his left and right flanks.
You must know his hierarchy.
You must know the way in.
You must know where different people are stationed.
You must demand this information from your spies.

10You want to know the enemy spies in order to convert
them into your men.
You must find sources of information and bribe them.
You must bring them in with you.
You must obtain them as double agents and use them as
your emissaries.

14Do this correctly and carefully.
You can contact both local and inside spies and obtain their
support.
Do this correctly and carefully.
You create doomed spies by deceiving professionals.
You can use them to give false information.
Do this correctly and carefully.
You must have surviving spies capable of bringing you infor-
mation at the right time.

4 You may want to address a certain market.
You may want to go after a specific business.
You may want to contact a certain decision-maker.
You must first know who the decision-makers are.
You must know their assistants.
You must know their organization.
You must know how to reach them.
You must know who influences their decisions.
You must get this information from your questions.

You must know how to get close to the key people within the customer's organization.
You must give them a reason to help you.
You must win them over to your side.
You must ask value questions to learn what is important to them and their company.

You must do this carefully.
You can ask qualifying and identifying questions to learn more about the customer.
You must also do this carefully.
You can ask leading questions.
You can use them to guide a person's thinking.
You must do this carefully as well.
You will then know how to ask closing questions at the appropriate time.

²¹These are the five different types of intelligence work.
You must be certain to master them all.
You must be certain to create double agents.
You cannot afford to be too cost conscious in creating these double agents.

This technique created the success of ancient Shang. 5
This is how the Shang held their dynasty.

³You must always be careful of your success.
Learn from Lu Ya of Shang.

⁵Be a smart commander and a good general.
You do this by using your best and brightest people for spying.
This is how you achieve the greatest success.
This is how you meet the necessities of war.
The whole army's position and ability to move depends on these spies.

◆ ◆ ◆

◆ ◆ ◆

There are five different types of questions.
You must be certain to master them all.
You must be certain to ask value questions.
You cannot invest too much time in understanding your customers' values.

5 Asking the right questions was the source of all past fortunes.
It is how those fortunes were maintained.

You must be concerned about your own success.
Learn from the successes of the past.

As a salesperson, you must keep your company informed.
You must use your best ideas and efforts to gather information.
This is how you make the biggest sales.
This is how you meet your company's needs.
Everything you do in the sales process depends upon the questions you've asked.

Index of Topics in *The Art of War*

This index identifies significant topics, keyed to the chapters, block numbers (big numbers in text), and line numbers (tiny numbers). The format is chapter:block.lines.

About the Translator and Author

Gary Gagliardi is recognized as America's leading expert on Sun Tzu's *The Art of War*. An award-winning author and businessperson, he is known for his ability to put sophisticated concepts into simple, easy-to-understand terms. He appears on hundreds of talk shows nationwide, providing strategic insight on the breaking news.

Gary began studying the Chinese classic more than thirty years ago, applying its principles first to his own career, then to building a successful business, and finally in training the world's largest organizations to be more competitive. He has spoken all over the world on a variety of topics concerning competition, from modern technology to ancient history. His books have been translated into many languages, including Japanese, Korean, Russian, and Spanish.

Gary began using Sun Tzu's competitive principles in a successful corporate career but soon started his own software company. In 1990, he wrote his first *Art of War* adaptation for his company's salespeople. By 1992, his company was one of *Inc.* magazine's 500 fastest-growing privately held companies in America. After he won the U.S. Chamber of Commerce **Blue Chip Quality Award** and became an Ernst and Young **Entrepreneur of the Year** finalist, his customers—AT&T, GE, and Motorola, among others—began inviting him to speak at their conferences. Jardin's, the original Hong Kong trading company known as "The Noble House," became one of his partners and even gave him the honor of firing the noontime cannon in Hong Kong's harbor. After becoming a multimillionaire when he sold his software company in 1997, he continued teaching *The Art of War* around the world.

Gary has authored several breakthrough works on *The Art of War*. In 1999, he translated each Chinese character to demonstrate its equation-like symmetry. In 2003, his work *The Art of War Plus The Ancient Chinese Revealed* won the **Independent Publishers Book Award** as the year's best new multicultural nonfiction work. In 2004, his adaptation of Sun Tzu's principles to marketing, *The Art of War Plus The Art of Marketing*, was selected as one of the three best business books by the **Ben Franklin Book Awards committee**. In 2004, he released a new work that explains the many hidden aspects of Sun Tzu's text, *The Art of War Plus Its Amazing Secrets*, which was selected as a **Highlighted Title** by Independent Publishers.

Gary has also written a large number of other adaptations of *The Art of War*, applying Sun Tzu's methods to wide variety of specific challenges.

Gary lives near Seattle with his wife.

Art of War Gift Books

The Mastering Strategy Series

^{Sun Tzu's} The Art of War Plus The Ancient Chinese Revealed
See the original! Each original Chinese character individually translated.

^{Sun Tzu's} The Art of War Plus Its Amazing Secrets
Learn the hidden secrets! The deeper meaning of *bing-fa* explained.

The Warrior Class: 306 Lessons in Strategy
The complete study guide! The most extensive analysis of *The Art of War* ever written.

Career and Business Series

^{Sun Tzu's} The Art of War Plus The Art of Career Building
For everyone! Use Sun Tzu's lessons to advance your career.

^{Sun Tzu's} The Art of War Plus The Art of Sales
For salespeople! Use Sun Tzu's lessons to win sales and keep customers.

^{Sun Tzu's} The Art of War Plus The Art of Management
For managers! Use Sun Tzu's lessons one managing teams more effectively.

^{Sun Tzu's} The Art of War Plus Strategy for Sales Managers
For managers! Use Sun Tzu's lessons to direct salespeople more effectively.

^{Sun Tzu's} The Art of War Plus The Art of Small Business
For business owners! Use Sun Tzu's lessons in building your own business.

^{Sun Tzu's} The Art of War Plus The Art of Marketing
For marketing professionals! Use Sun Tzu's lessons to win marketing warfare.

Life Strategies Series

^{Sun Tzu's} The Art of War Plus The Warrior's Apprentice
A first book of strategy for young adults.

^{Sun Tzu's} The Art of War Plus The Art of Love
For lifelong love! *Bing-fa* applied to finding, winning, and keeping love alive.

^{Sun Tzu's} The Art of War Plus The Art of Parenting Teens
For every parent! Strategy applied to protecting, guiding, and motivating teens.

Current Events Series

^{Sun Tzu's} The Art of War Plus Strategy against Terror
An examination of the War on Terror using Sun Tzu's timeless principles.

Audio and Video

Amazing Secrets of The Art of War: Audio with book
1 1/2 Hours 2 CD set

Amazing Secrets of *The Art of War:* Video with book
1 1/2 Hours VHS

To Order On-line: Visit www.BooksOnStrategy.com
Fax Orders: 206-546-9756. Voice: 206-533-9357.